Routledge Revivals

God and Mammon

First published in 1931, this is an attempt by the great economist J. A. Hobson to analyse the relations between economics and religion. After considering the origins of the conflicts and compromises between God and Mammon in the life of primitive man, the author concerns himself primarily with medieval and modern Christianity and the business climate and ethos corresponding with these periods. In particular he focuses upon Catholicism and Protestantism, before considering the attitude of the church towards modern economic movements.

T0361972

God and Mammon

The Relations of Religion and Economics

J. A. Hobson

Routledge
Taylor & Francis Group

First published in 1931
by C. A. Watts & Co Ltd

This edition first published in 2011 by Routledge
2 Park Square, Milton Park, Abingdon, Oxon, OX14 4RN

Simultaneously published in the USA and Canada
by Routledge
711 Third Avenue, New York, NY 10017

Routledge is an imprint of the Taylor & Francis Group, an informa business

Publisher's Note
The publisher has gone to great lengths to ensure the quality of this
reprint but points out that some imperfections in the original copies may
be apparent.

Disclaimer
The publisher has made every effort to trace copyright holders and
welcomes correspondence from those they have been unable to contact.

A Library of Congress record exists under LC Control Number: 32000088

ISBN 13: 978-0-415-69990-7 (hbk)
ISBN 13: 978-0-203-12741-4 (ebk)
ISBN 13: 978-0-415-50595-6 (pbk)

The Forum Series.—No. 13.

GOD AND MAMMON

THE RELATIONS OF
RELIGION AND ECONOMICS

BY
J. A. HOBSON

London :
WATTS & CO.,
5 & 6 johnson's court, fleet street, f.c.4

FIRST PUBLISHED, JUNE 1931

PRINTED AND PUBLISHED IN GREAT BRITAIN FOR THE RATIONALIST PRESS
ASSOCIATION LIMITED BY C. A. WATTS & CO. LIMITED, 5 & 6 JOHNSON'S
COURT, FLEET STREET, LONDON, E.C. 4

PREFACE

THIS brief attempt at an intelligible analysis and survey of the relations between economics and religion has some difficulties to encounter. Even had I possessed the necessary knowledge, spacial limits would have precluded an extension of my enquiry into all or most of the great religions of the world. Even the most condensed statement of facts in so many fields would have left no scope for the necessary interpretation.

Under such circumstances it seemed best, after a short preliminary chapter dealing with the beginnings of the conflicts and compromises of God and Mammon as shown in the life of primitive man, to confine myself to selected studies in medieval and modern Christianity, and in the business life coeval with these religious phases, so as to bring out most clearly the mingled aspects of discord and harmony.

Particular attention is given to the attitude adopted towards modern business life by what Matthew Arnold termed " the Protestantism of the Protestant Religion " as illustrated in the Calvinist churches of Western Europe, in Wesleyanism, among Baptists and Quakers, chiefly in Britain and the United States. The material aid rendered by God and Mammon to one another in the pursuit of this world's goods demands a closer psychological analysis than has here been possible. But I take it to be a main purpose of this Forum Series to stimulate thought and evoke study in many readers. Though an increasing volume of attention has in recent years been devoted to the relation between Capitalism and Religion, some of the richest fields still remain unexplored. Readers of this essay will readily recognise how deep a debt I owe to Mr. R. H. Tawney's work, *Religion and the Rise of Capitalism*, as well as to several other recent writers.

J. A. H.

February, 1931

CONTENTS

CHAPTER I

Economics in Primitive Religions

PRIMITIVE man cannot be properly described as either an economic or a religious being. But in his earliest history we can discern in him groups of instinctive and conscious urges and activities which led him later on to the distinction between the satisfaction of his bodily needs and that of his spiritual needs. From the beginning both the opposition and the co-operation of economics and religion, God and Mammon, were latent in man's life. We see him, first, an animal among other animals, seeking to eat and to avoid being eaten, superior to other animals in using and making shelter, and in getting weapons, tools, coverings, and ornaments from the material of his environment, instead of growing them as parts of his body. Thus forced to explore the place in which he lives, in order to utilize its resources for the protection of himself and his species, he comes to realize nature as containing powers partly friendly, partly hostile, to his life. His dawning imagination dwells more upon the irregular and hostile activities of nature than upon the normal and friendly ones. Storms, pestilences, droughts, famines, floods, and other perilous eccentricities of nature work powerfully upon his mind. He easily comes to attribute such happenings to inimical powers inhabiting and moving natural objects, which must be circumvented or appeased. His early endeavours to influence nature were not by methods we can call religious. He did not at first conceive nature as operated by gods or other beings like himself though stronger. But he recognized forces of nature that might be affected favourably in their working by what we call Magic. Frazer, in his great study, *The Golden Bough*, distinguishes two sorts of Magic— imitative and contagious. You could get rain by pouring some water on the ground, giving " the tip," so to speak, to the clouds, or you could injure your enemy by getting possession of a bit of him, his hair or nail clippings, or by making an image of him, or even by the injurious use of his name.

1

But not everyone knew enough of the mysterious ways of nature to do such things successfully. So in a tribe the magician, witch doctor, or wizard would gain recognition as an expert, knowing and influencing the ways of nature. Such magic may be accounted the beginning both of science and religion, which for some little distance went hand-in-hand together.

Doubtless the keener imagination of certain men came very early to endow the forces of nature with wills, desires, and purposes like those they felt working in themselves, and with some sort of person operating them. So came animism, a sort of half-way house on the road to definite religion. Some anima, or spirit, inhabited each bit of organic nature; each tree or shrub, and all moving objects of inorganic nature, stars, ocean, rivers, the very earth itself, were the residence of some ruling spirit. Though fear was the chief begetter of religion,[1] it was not the only ingredient in early religious belief and emotion. The survival of the souls of the dead in some sort of existence was an early widespread belief; and some reverent regard tempered the fear which doubtless predominated among the survivors who " worshipped " these ancestors. Nor can we disregard some sentiment of the sublime and beautiful in the feelings of early man towards the most impressive beings in nature. As personification became more distinct, we cannot wonder that the sun, the moon, mother-earth and her generative powers became objects of worship, chiefly for the benefits they could confer upon or withhold from man, but also on their own account for the majesty of their form and power.

We get a strong touch of this sentiment in the language Milton puts into the mouth of Satan :—

> Oh, thou who with surpassing beauty crown'd
> Lookst from thy sole dominion like the God
> Of this new earth—on thee I call.

But early worship was predominantly fear, and continued to be so through the development of what are called the higher religions. Indeed, modern Christianity, though sometimes telling its followers that " God is love," still speaks of a devout Christian as a god-fearing, not a god-loving, man.

Man's discovery or invention of divine beings peopling and conducting nature is seen to be itself a very natural process.

[1] Mr. Warde Fowler, in his *Social Life of Rome* (p. 343), speaks of " this feeling of fear or nervousness which lies at the root of the meaning of the word *religio*."

As animism replaced cruder magic in the human interpretation of natural forces, it fell to the priest, or priest-king, to displace the magician, and to gather into his hands the fear, reverence, and regard due to one who knew how to conciliate the Higher Powers. The multiplicity of private local godlets grew into a hierarchy of potentates, as wider communications enlarged the smaller tribal life, or conquest placed an invading people's gods in a higher spiritual status than those of the conquered people.

It is not my concern here to attempt to trace the separate or mingled growth of the great religions in Babylon, Sumeria, Assyria, India, and Egypt, with the various changing rituals of prayer and sacrifice. My task is to try to indicate the relations of interdependence and opposition between the material and spiritual aspects of human life, as they show themselves in the evolution of economic processes on the one hand, and of religious institutions on the other.

The story of God and Mammon is largely, but not wholly, an economic interpretation of history. For throughout human history it has always been difficult to distinguish the economic from the other vital activities of man. Strictly speaking, the economic life does not arise until trading has begun, with some division of labour yielding to each man a surplus of certain goods beyond his own needs, which he can exchange for the surpluses of other goods belonging to other men. Even after this division or specialization of labour, with exchange of surplus, has come about, a good deal of useful and even necessary work is done within the home, on which no price is set, and which does not enter into economic reckoning. Until money has come into general use for the appraisal and exchange of goods and services, wealth as an economic term continues to be vague, and much serviceable energy still lies outside the category of " economic." In primitive life most of man's efforts must be devoted to maintaining the life of the individual, the family, and the tribe. Most thinking and planning, as well as action, were devoted to this end. Hunter, fisher, farmer, fighter, seek to get food and protection for their folk from the natural environment, or by robbery and conquest. Magic first, afterwards religion, was invoked to assist them in these vitally necessary tasks. " In primitive society, where uniformity of occupation is the rule, and the distribution of the community into various classes of workers has hardly begun, every man is more or less his own magician ; he practises charms and incantations for his own good and the injury of his enemies. But a great step in advance has been taken when a special class of magicians has been instituted; when, in other words, a number of men have been set apart for the express purpose of benefiting the whole community by their skill, whether that skill be directed to the healing of diseases, the regulation of the weather, or any other object of general utility." [1]   When magic passed through the animist stage into religion, and priesthoods provided themselves with sacred groves, shrines, temples, and the proper trappings of a deity, no essential change took place in the relations between the material and the spiritual life.

These relations were very close. The magician, priest, or priest-king, possessing spiritual influence with a great god, or himself a god, was the first professional parasite, the first person capable of living upon the products of other people's labour, whether bestowed as voluntary gifts, blackmail, or sacrifices to the gods. His was a perilous life. For the reverence and sanctity accorded to him as representative of the god were easily upset. In a very real sense his income was " payment by results." He must deliver the goods, produce rain or fair weather when needed for the crops, stop pestilences and other troubles. Something could be done by skilled prophecy—e.g., he could " produce " rain when rain was coming, and perform effective rites of fertilization in springtime. But any calamitous failure was taken to prove incapacity or malice. On such occasions you would beat your god, or put to death his minister. In some ways primitive religion was more sincere than ours. We still pray for rain and for good harvests, but we do not kill our parsons when their prayers fail.

Not only primitive man, but civilized peoples, who had invented tools to aid their labour, still recognized their dependence upon the natural resources and the fecundity of nature for their successful livelihood. It is not too much to say that this fecundity of nature was the first consideration in the great religions of the world, whether of Ra, Zeus, Ammon, Mithra, or some other Sun-god, or some female deity of fertility such as Cybele or Ceres. Even where, as among the Celts, official religion was solar, all their chief festivals relating to points in the sun's progress during the year, this sun-worship cannot be detached from the worshipful regard to the generative processes in the vegetable and animal world. Earth was conceived as the mother-element, and the idea of the mother-goddess prevailed in ancient times from India to Ireland.

[1] Frazer, *The Golden Bough*, Abridged Edition, p. 61.

The account given in *The Golden Bough* of the worship of Adonis indicates how far the older magic had survived in the early religions of the East. The " gardens of Adonis " were " baskets or pots filled with earth, in which wheat, barley, lettuces, fennel, and various kinds of flowers were sown and tended for eight days, chiefly or exclusively by women. Fostered by the sun's heat, the plants shot up rapidly; but, having no root, they withered as rapidly away, and at the end of eight days were carried out with the images of the dead Adonis, and flung with them into the sea or into springs." "The rapid growth of the wheat and barley in the gardens of Adonis was intended to make the corn shoot up; and the throwing of the gardens and the images into the water was a charm to secure a due supply of fertilizing rain." [1]

In India, Sicily, Sardinia, the custom still survives, though in the two latter countries St. John has replaced Adonis, and the Easter celebration of the dead and risen Christ has been grafted on to the earlier ritual in celebration of the dead and risen Adonis.

If these early religions were definitely directed to aid man in what may be called his economic purposes, through bringing spiritual influences to bear upon crops and herds and other requisites of life, a new potent economic situation arose. To the priesthood in charge of the shrines or temples a large part of the " surplus " wealth of the people passed. Not only gifts of food and sacrificial offerings came to them in order to win the favour of the god or avert his ill-will, but the temples soon began to be used as treasuries in which durable articles of value, gold, silver, precious stones, objects of art, could find a secure resting-place. Where, as in Egypt or Babylon, the material arts of civilization enabled much slave or other labour to be applied to the production of these luxuries, the safest repositories of such wealth were the palaces and tombs of god-kings, or the temples of their priests.

Here religion was able to exercise a double influence upon economic life—first, to extract " for services rendered " a large and increasing share of the growing " surplus " wealth of a rising civilization with improving arts of production; secondly, to safeguard such stored treasures by the religious sentiment which in an age of violence protected them against sacrilegious pillage. Thieves would not break through and steal; even invaders sometimes spared the shrines of alien

[1] Frazer, *op. cit.* p. 341.

but recognized deities.[1] When valuable metals became the medium of purchase and exchange the temples became the most available storehouses. Indeed, Mr. A. R. Burns [2] says that silver from the temple hoard was put into circulation to facilitate trade, as notes are now withdrawn from the banks. Again, a closer early connection between God and Mammon is suggested by Mr. Hawtrey, who tells us [3] that " the word ' money ' is believed to be derived from Moneta, an attribute of the Roman goddess Juno, because the ancient Roman mint was established in the temple of Juno Moneta." Though much treasure became the property of the temple or its priesthood, there is evidence that kings made use of the temples to keep metallic reserves in the shape of bars of gold, silver, or valuable metals against the needs of wartime or other emergencies, placing them under the protection of the gods. The ordinary Greek temple contained a treasury building for the deposit of local offerings, as did the shrines of Olympia and Delphi on a larger national scale.[4]

Thus we find from the earliest times in various countries of the ancient world a reciprocity of services between God and Mammon—religion and industry. The gods gave protection against enemies in war, promoted vegetation and animal fertility, and gave " luck " in hunting, fishing, and agriculture. In return, the priests got treasures for their temples, food and other necessaries and comforts for themselves, including as a rule male and female slaves for their support and enjoyment. In Asiatic and African countries, where slave labour was abundant under despotic rule, a large and increasing part of such treasure as did not rust or decay came to be deposited in the temples. This was certainly the case in Egypt, Babylon, Chaldea, Syria, India, and to a less extent in Greece, where

[1] In Italy, where brigandage was bolder than elsewhere, holiness was not always a sufficient protection, for Cicero tells of thefts of statues and other temple property (de Natura Deorum, i, 29. 52).

[2] *Money and Monetary Policy in Early Times.*

[3] Article " Money " in *Encyclopædia Britannica.*

[4] The Chapel or Chamber of the Pyx of Westminster Abbey, which forms part of Edward the Confessor's monastic building, though originally used as a chapel, became later the Abbots' Treasury, and many sacred relics were preserved there. Subsequently it became the depository of the " pyx " or box containing the Exchequer trialplates of gold and silver used as standards of reference at the periodical tests of the weight and fineness of the coins of the realm. These tests, known as " trials of the pyx," were held at Westminster till 1842. At the Dissolution the Chapel of the Pyx (the Abbots' Treasury), with the Chapter House and the Royal Treasury below it, were retained under Royal jurisdiction, and are still under the charge, not of the Abbey authorities, but of the officials of the Palace of Westminster.

slave labour was less abundant. The wealth and leisure thus secured to the temples and the priestly castes stimulated among them the beginnings of culture in literature, science, and the fine arts of music, architecture, sculpture, painting, dancing, thus laying the foundations of many of the higher crafts and industries that spread in secular life.

In thus presenting the early relations of God and Mammon in the light of reciprocity of services, we cannot, however, ignore the fact that whereas the Mammon, typifying wealth and industry, played his part fairly, making good and abundant payment at the holy shrines, the god's priestly representatives rendered no substantial services in return, unless we conceive any sort of belief in higher powers to be better than none. Though the believers in these gods doubtless regarded themselves as getting a real "quid pro quo," when, in return for gifts and sacrifices, the priests undertook to procure the aid or avert the hostility of the gods, the fact that these religious goods were not genuine is a highly relevant consideration in our thesis. Perhaps still more important is the well-attested fact that, while the ordinary priest or soothsayer, accepting easily the current traditions, was sincere in holding that his performance of ritual was actually serviceable in influencing gods, the keener-witted members of the priesthood were often sceptics, and secretly derided the ceremonial dupery they practised. Augur winked to augur, as they passed.

Though occasionally bolder sceptics became open heretics and reformers, many more remained at their profitable posts, as hypocrites. For open sceptics and nonconformists were not tolerated in times when kings were gods or demi-gods, and when questioning accepted religious rites was treason as well as sacrilege. The gravest moral damage of these religions consisted, not in the fact that their deities were unreal and so incapable of performing the high functions ascribed to them, but in that the minds of the most intelligent men of the ages were poisoned by consciously false conformity. Sincerity in belief is always a matter of degree, and, while few priests in primitive or even more civilized communities may have been clear-eyed sceptics, many must have kept on smothering doubts about the efficacy of their rituals, thus debasing the moral currency of their society.

The less sincere the religious professions that they held, the laxer their creed, the more rigorous would be their addiction to the worldly contacts which enabled those who had renounced treasures in another world to accumulate treasures in this. If the successful researches into the material remains of Ur of the Chaldees, Thebes, Babylon, or Crete could lay open the psychology of the priesthood in their shrines and temples, it would furnish a wealth of mingled " rationalization " and hypocrisy even more deserving of attention than the products of art and industry which surprise our world to-day.

CHAPTER II

Catholicism and Economic Life

SO far we have treated the relations of God and Mammon as, upon the whole, those of co-operation and mutual support. But the attitude of conscious and intense conflict which appears in all the higher or more " spiritual " religions is of equal importance. In all the early religions these elements of conflict are apt to appear. The fear of unknown powers, the importance of omens, portents, dreams, faith in some personal immortality, the " sinfulness of sin," a glimpse of order in the universe and the image of some great director of this order—such thoughts and emotions, aroused in more sensitive minds, induced " reformers " to set up a sharp opposition between the material and a spiritual world, between the good of the body and that of the soul. The habit of dwelling upon higher powers of nature, conceived as deities, and the power of the human mind or spirit to influence or control the body, led earnest prophets in all ages to favour a valuation of life and character in which things of the body should be subordinate to things of the spirit. The ascetic life plays so important a part in our later religious movements that its persistent recurrence in human history deserves special note. Whenever a religion got to be a dominant factor in a growing civilisation, it became, as we have seen, entangled with concerns of Mammon, and worldly power and riches began to subjugate the more spiritual or intellectual aspects of its creed. Some priest, or saint, or prophet, might then arise, with personality and prestige sufficient to lead a spiritual revolt, and to produce a reformation or a new faith. Such protests were raised by Isaiah, Ezekiel, and other prophets against the formalism and materialism into which Judaism had fallen. In substance such revolts were an invitation to renounce Mammon, and to concentrate upon the worship of a mystic divinity, to give up the sacrifices which could be of no value to a spiritual being, and to substitute a devout obedience to his moral laws.

In Hebraism these recurrent revolts against worldliness

were the more significant because of the special claim of Jehovah-worship to be a purely spiritual religion, both in its ritual and in the benefits accruing to its worshippers. It is clear that Christianity in its beginning was one of these revolts, an attempt to clean up the professionalism and the commercialism which had seized the seat of worship at Jerusalem. The action, imputed to Jesus, of expelling the money-changers from the precincts of the Temple, gives a dramatic expression to the encroachment of Mammon upon the spirituality of the Hebrew religion. The main tenor of the Gospel teaching is a plea for a return to a way of living which should keep under the body and its claims, and concentrate men's thoughts and activities upon a holy life. All the characteristic qualities of the Jew as business man, his skilful profiteering as trader and money-lender, his steady pursuit of gain by careful planning, hard bargaining, and usurious loans, were subjects of repeated condemnation. To despise riches, to take no thought for the morrow, to give to all who ask, seeking nothing in return, and to find perfection in selling all you have and giving to the poor—such precepts were an express repudiation of all partnership with Mammon.

It is no doubt true that Jesus confronted a state of society in which commercialism and industrialism were in their infancy, a peasant and small-town community where the economic problems which confront us did not arise. But, because Jesus had little to say about trade morals, it by no means follows that professing Christians of later times are justified in holding that his express teaching upon the duty of a man towards his neighbour in the simple society of his time can be set aside as irrelevant to the consideration of the business ethics of our time. " It is far wiser," writes a modern critic,[1] " to recognize frankly the fact that just as Jesus' teaching is non-political, so it is in any strict sense non-economic." Such a judgment destroys the unity of the moral life. The effect of accepting it would be to confine the teaching of the founder of Christianity to considerations of a private personality which has no existence.

In the earliest Christian communities a virtual communism prevailed, though the precise nature of the community of property is a subject of controversy. " A more careful examination of the passages in the Acts," writes Dr. Carlyle,[2] " shows clearly enough that this was no systematic division of property, but that the charitable instinct of the infant

[1] Shailer Matthew, *Jesus on Social Institutions*.
[2] Quoted by O'Brien, *Medieval Economic Teaching*, p. 44.

Church was so great that those who were in want were completely supported by those who were more prosperous. . . . Still there was no systematic communism, no theory of the necessity of it." While there are passages in the writings of the early Fathers which seem to point otherwise, such as Tertullian's statement : " One in mind and soul, we do not hesitate to share our earthly goods with one another. All things are common among us but our wives "—it is pretty clear that private ownership was not discarded, even in the period when the early expectation of Christ's second coming would make the brief possession of earthly goods a matter of slight importance. As time went on, the attitude of the Church towards property became a matter of casuistry, resting on a basic distinction between divine and human right. Here is St. Augustine : " By what right does every man possess what he possesses ? Is it not by human right ? For by divine right ' the earth is the Lord's and the fulness thereof.' The poor and the rich God made of one clay : the same earth supports alike the poor and the rich. By human right, however, one says, ' This estate is mine.' By human right, therefore, is by right of the Emperor. Why so ? Because God has distributed to mankind these very human rights, through the emperors and kings of the world.'

A singular bit of sophistry, which recognizes Roman emperors as the instruments of God, and in effect abolishes the distinction between divine and human right ! But no doubt it expresses the renewed desire of the established Church to come to terms with Mammon. We soon begin to enter upon the special line of defence of property characteristic of the Church up to the present day, and well expressed by Hilary of Pocitina : [1] " To possess riches is not wrongful, but rather the manner in which possession is used "—not the manner in which possession is obtained !

Liberalitas, always recognized as a virtue that redeems ownership, does not, however, consist merely in distributing to others. For we are told that " a wise and prudent saving of money for investment would be considered a course of conduct within the meaning of the term *liberalitas*, especially if the enterprise in which the money were invested were one which would benefit the community as a whole." [2]

But the chief interest of a study of the economics of the Roman Church as it gained control of Western Europe lies in the conflict between its ethical principles as enumerated by Aquinas and other leading schoolmen and the business practices

[1] Quoted by O'Brien, p. 60. [2] *Idem*, p. 73.

B

which it was induced to sanction and to follow. "The most fundamental difference between medieval and modern economic thought," writes Mr. Tawney,[1] "consists, indeed, in the fact that, whereas the latter normally refers to economic expediency, however it may be interpreted, for the justification of any particular action, policy, or system of organization, the former starts from the position that there is a moral authority to which considerations of economic expediency must be subordinated. The practical application of this conception is the attempt to try every transaction by a rule of right which is largely, though not wholly, independent of the fortuitous combinations of economic circumstances."

The "just price" which is the basic expression of this "rule of right" is soon discovered to be little more than a pious aspiration, inapplicable to any actual market. What was the criterion of justice? The schoolmen of the fourteenth century soon found themselves enmeshed in the controversy which divided our nineteenth-century economists, as to whether the cost of the producer or the utility of the consumer was the true source of value. Some of them reached the futile judgment that a "fair price" was reached under freedom of contract, a view which only transferred the difficulty from a definition of "justice" to a definition of "freedom." Their analysis soon led them to allow for varying circumstances of scarcity, and we learn that St. Antonino, writing in the fifteenth century, when commerce was already highly developed, came to the conclusion that "the fairness of a price could at best be a matter only of 'probability and conjecture,' since it would vary with places, periods, and persons."[2] A very reasonable conclusion, but one that reduces to nullity the principle it professes to expound.

But however faulty the theory of the "just price," it is probable that the early influence of Canon Law in endeavouring to apply it was of considerable service in checking gross abuses of economic force. For free and equal markets were rare, the monopoly of local guilds everywhere confronting the consumer.

This same economic situation helps to explain the immense attention paid to the principle and practice of "usury." Though capitalism in overseas trade and in a few developing industries was beginning to make progress and to use co-operative capital, most borrowing and lending of money had relation to the personal needs and misfortunes of the borrower, when in bargaining with lenders he was at a grave disadvantage. For in small local communities his plight was known to the

---

[1] *Religion and the Rise of Capitalism*, p. 40.   [2] *Idem*, p. 40.

lender, and could be converted into an instrument of extortion, as still continues to be the case in primitive societies.

" Usury," as condemned by the medieval Church, did not signify, as now, an excessive rate of interest on a loan. All interest, regarded as a fixed payment stipulated in advance for the loan of money, was usury. In an age when there was little or no scope for the employment of money in ordinary business, and when any surplus income was therefore conceived as lying idle in its owner's stocking or strong-box, it did not seem unreasonable to expect that a neighbour's temporary need should be met by lending without interest such otherwise idle money. If the lender had full security for getting it back when he needed it, that sufficed. And from the earliest times compensation was allowed against such failure to repay. There were other special qualifications of the main principle. Any gain which the lender may forgo, or any loss he may incur, as the result of his lending, he may recover in payment. If the loan be to a landowner, he may take a share of the produce of the soil, for this is in part, at any rate, nature's work. But he has no claim to any gain which the borrower may make out of his own labour assisted by the loan, for this product proceeds from the labour alone—not a very reasonable view, but one which seemed to fit the simple economic situation of the time.

It is hardly necessary to add that the condemnation of money-lending (even with the qualifications I have specified) did not apply to large financial operations conducted by the rich and great. Kings and feudal nobles borrowed for their war needs and their extravagances from the international money market long organized in Italy, Germany, and later in Holland. The Church itself, in the person of the Pope, regularly employed these finance-houses for lending or for borrowing, and even used threats of excommunication as a means of enforcing interest payments. Protests were made from time to time by moralists against such discrimination, but in vain. For, as capitalism developed in the later Middle Ages, the common sense of most Catholic communities recognized that the strict enforcement of such principles would hamper business and was opposed to the interests alike of borrower and lender.

For our purpose it remains significant that ecclesiastical law, as expressed in the Canons of the Church, continued, even after the Reformation, to claim and exercise jurisdiction over certain orders of cases of money-lending in this country.

Summarising the claim of the Church in medieval times to

have exerted a humanizing influence over economic life, we may in general agree with Mr. Tawney's contention that " in the earlier Middle Ages it had stood for the protection of peaceful labour, for the care of the poor, the unfortunate, and the oppressed—for the ideal, at least, of social solidarity against the naked force of violence and oppression." [1] But, as he himself admits, the Church not only recognized, but enforced serfdom, while ecclesiastical landlords were neither better nor worse than others in their treatment of their serfs. Nor was the care of the poor exercised in any efficiently organized system of charity. The fact is that the Church came easily to acquiesce in all the major inequalities, injustices, and oppressions of the economic system, when the beneficiaries of such system were the rich, the great, the powerful, or itself. Indeed, the Church did not merely acquiesce in serfdom as practised under the custom of most feudal societies. It expressly endorsed and upheld the ownership of man by man, slavery, as a legitimate form of property. The *Catholic Encyclopedia* thus expresses itself on the subject :

" Christian teachers, following the example of St. Paul, implicitly accept slavery as not in itself incompatible with the Christian law. The Apostle counsels slaves to obey their masters and to bear with their conditions patiently. This estimate of slavery continued to prevail until it became fixed in the systematized ethical teaching of the schools; and so it remained without any conspicuous alteration until the end of the eighteenth century." [2]

Indeed, a moral justification for slavery was provided by St. Augustine, who held that " it was one of the penalties incurred by man as a result of the sin of Adam and Eve." Nay, further, we learn from St. Chrysostom that " slavery was declared to be a blessing because, like poverty, it afforded the opportunity of practising the virtues of humility and patience." [3]

So much for the Church's " care of the poor, the unfortunate, and the oppressed."

It is evident that the Christianity of the Church never seriously attempted to apply the plain principles of the teaching of the Gospels to the economic life of the peoples. If they had taken the line that such secular activities lay outside their province, and that religion was entirely concerned with the spiritual preparation for another life, the truckling

---

[1] *Religion and the Rise of Capitalism*, p. 63.
[2] Article " Slavery " in *Catholic Encyclopedia*.
[3] Cf. O'Brien, *op. cit.* p. 92.

to Mammon might have been avoided. But taking, as it did, the whole area of economic conduct under the diocese of its spiritual authority, its actual policy must be deemed one of continual concessions to the lust of power and greed of gain which assumed increased rule over economic life as the simpler orders of primitive industry yielded to the complexity of modern methods of production and of markets, and to the displacement of custom and status by the greed and conflict of competitive enterprise.

This judgment, however, may reasonably be contested by those who take a more objective view of economic progress. A serious attempt to apply the principle of " the just price " and a condemnation of " usury " would assuredly have crippled the adventure in competitive industry and the widening of markets that were essential to the increase of wealth and the rising standard of life in the later Middle Ages. If some of the attendant evils of unbridled avarice might have been checked, it would have been by maintaining an unenlightened repression of the new economic forces whose free expression made for the general gain of the community in the long run.

*　　*　　*

The Catholic Church might, however, have won more sympathy for its efforts to maintain its spiritual control over the economic world if it had kept its own hands clean from the sin of avarice which it so harshly condemned in others. But a study of the doctrines and practices employed by the Church bring to light what we may call an esoteric economic system, by means of which it fastened suckers into the minds of its adherents, so as to extract from them an increasing share of any wealth they might acquire.

The most potent instrument in this economic system was the doctrine of Purgatory. The belief in a post-mortem period of spiritual cleansing is by no means a peculiar invention of Christianity. It may, indeed, be claimed as a humane provision for a spiritual eternal life, though painful in its actual incidence; for, according to the best authorities, souls during their sojourn in Purgatory were tormented by material fire. But the points in the doctrine that are of focal interest for our enquiry are two : First, a limited period of time is set upon the suffering; secondly, this period may be shortened or even cancelled by certain interventions of the Church, induced by acts of piety on the part of believers.

Now it is easy to recognize what a powerful instrument was thus placed at the disposal of the Church. A spiritual power in the first instance, but easily convertible into an economic power. There is no ground for holding that in its original discovery of Purgatory the Church realized the economic potency of this doctrine, or saw in it the source of wealth which it became. It was in all probability the sense of power, rather than of wealth, which first led to the development of the doctrine. If Purgatory had remained a fixity in the divine plan, there would have been nothing in it for the Church. But it is evident from the very weakness of the scriptural basis of the doctrine that the Church early recognized its practical potency. Its main reliance was upon a passage in the gospel of Matthew [1] stating that "whosoever speaketh against the Holy Ghost, it shall not be forgiven him, neither in this world, neither in the world to come." This, St. Augustine argued, signifies that the statement that "some sinners are not forgiven either in this world or the next, would not be truly said unless there were other (sinners) who, though not forgiven in this world, are forgiven in the next." [2]

But God will not be moved to remission of any penalty by the merits of the deceased or by pity for his suffering! Motives must be applied from outside. What motives? Augustine says "the prayers and alms of the faithful, the Holy Sacrifice of the Altar, aid the faithful departed and *move the Lord* to deal with them in mercy and kindness, and this is the practice of the universal Church handed down by the Fathers."

Now from earliest times Prayers for the Dead were closely linked up with Purgatory. But this private piety of the friends and relatives of the deceased would be found far less potent than the Holy Sacrifice of the Altar, the performance of the Mass. The superior efficacy of this act was early recognized in the leaving of sums of money by dying persons for the purpose, or by contributions from attendants at the celebrations thus induced. Protests were made from time to time by churchmen scandalized by the venality of such conduct. "What, pray, is the cause why the other church services remain in the simplicity and purity of their first institution, and this alone (of the Mass) is doubled contrary to its first institution? Certainly the cause is in the offerings : for at the Mass we offer and at no other service." [3] From such

---

[1] Ch. xiii v. 32.
[2] A still feebler support to Purgatory is found in 1 Corinthians iii. 15.
[3] Petrus Cantor, cited G. G. Coulton, *Life of the Middle Ages*, Vol. I, p. 36.

offerings we learn " altars are erected, sanctuaries are adorned, and monasteries built." " Some again have invented a Mass for the slaughter of those lately slain round about Jerusalem, as of newly-made martyrs, by which Mass they think to entice to themselves the greater oblations by reason of the favour that men bear to such men slain (in the Crusades)."

The struggle of the puritan spirit against the encroach-ment of Mammon in the monastic life is well expressed by St. Bernard's rebuke to his fellow-Cistercians : " I marvel how monks could grow accustomed to such intemperance in eating and drinking, clothing and bedding, riding abroad and building, that, wheresoever those things are wrought most busily and with most pleasure and expense, there Religion is thought to be best kept." [1]

Each successive monastic order—Benedictine, Cluniac, Cistercian, Carthusian, Franciscan, Dominican—began with genuine professions of " poverty " and developed into an instrument for extracting wealth, which they applied, partly to fineries of architecture, partly to comfortable and luxurious living. How could it be otherwise with such a potent instrument as Purgatory in their possession ? To capitalize the fear of Purgatory seems a business policy which was natural and inevitable. Hell could not be profitably handled, for its pains were infinite, and a market needs the quality of scarcity. The limitation of Purgatory lent itself to an instalment system of selling exemptions from torment. Consider how great must have been the potency of this instru-ment when a baron on his death-bed was attended by a church-man able to reduce his approaching period of post-mortem agony by a thousand years, or even to cancel it, provided he would put his cross (he could not read or write !) to a prepared document conveying a large part of his estates to Holy Church, in the shape of the adjoining monastery or chantry.

But Purgatory was not the only instrument for extracting wealth from the faithful and the fearful. Selling the right to sin was another lucrative method. This went by the names of Indulgence and Pardon. In the official catechism of the Roman Church indulgence is defined as " the remission of the temporal punishment which often remains due to sin after its guilt has been forgiven." Such remission may be plenary or partial, according to the terms of the indulgence. In form it was a remission of private penances for sin granted by the Pope. In practice it was a retail purchase of the right to sin, a comparatively late development of spiritual economics.

[1] G. G. Coulton, *op. cit.*, Vol. IV, p. 139.

The first plenary indulgence was granted by Pope Urban II for the first Crusade, a very suitable occasion, for a good deal of hard sinning was associated with that historical episode. By the thirteenth century we learn that indulgences were in pretty general practice by all Churches, and lasted up to the later part of the sixteenth century. They brought into operation a profession of Pardoners, or collectors, who dealt with the matter on a sound business basis, though competition seems to have impaired the earlier monopoly-values. Piers Plowman spoke of pardoners who " give pardon for pence pound-meal about "—i.e., wholesale, and Pope Boniface IX complained of Pardoners " absolving even impenitent sinners for ridiculously small sums." In 1450 Thomas Gascoigne, Chancellor of Oxford University, wrote : " Sinners say nowadays ' I care not how many or how great sins I commit before God, for I shall easily and quickly get plenary remission of any guilt and penalty whatever by absolution and indulgence granted to me from the Pope, whose writing and grant I have bought for 4d. or 6d.—or for a game of tennis.' "

The use of indulgences, though primarily designed as a release from penance due for sins committed by the living, came to be extended to the case of souls in Purgatory. For we learn that " St. Thomas holds that indulgences avail principally for the person who performs the work for which the indulgence is given, but secondarily may avail even for the dead, if the form in which the indulgence is granted be so worded as to be capable of such interpretation," and he adds : " Nor is there any reason why the Church may not dispose of its treasure of merits in favour of the dead, as it surely dispenses it in favour of the living." [1]

The abuses of this power to sell the right to sin eventually became so flagrant that the Council of Trent in 1562 abolished the office of Pardoner. Other aspects of the business life of the Church are the uses of Saints for purposes of pilgrimages, the sale of relics, and the performance of miraculous cures. The most notorious example of this trade is found in the multiplication of pieces of the Cross. But probably by far the largest profit was obtained by coining the miraculous virtues of local Saints and Virgins and by selling objects which bore the virtues of contiguous magic.

That the better-conducted monasteries were seats of learning and homes of literary, artistic, and even scientific culture in a world of ignorance and gross materialism may well be conceded. It is often claimed that their sanctity enabled

[1] *Catholic Encyclopedia*, Vol. XII, p. 579.

the fine arts of life to survive during " the dark ages." But there is another side to this picture. For, if monasteries and nunneries attracted to themselves men and women of superior mental and moral refinement, their celibate life must be held responsible for a survival of the intellectually and morally unfit, and a loss to humanity of the stock which bore the promise of progress in individual ability and character. Such withdrawal from the world of so large a number of the finer-natured men and women must upon the whole be accounted among the gravest injuries inflicted by religion upon the progress of humanity.

Taking account, however, of the distinctively economic arts, the monasteries both here and on the continent are entitled to some credit for improvements in agriculture, building, weaving, and in other handicrafts withdrawn from the conservatism of the guilds. Even medicine and book-keeping seem to have owed much of their early cultivation to monastic life. But upon the whole the money-making proclivity of the organized Churches must be deemed to be as detrimental to the evolution of progressive industry as the ascetic spirit which inspired the early anchorites, and to which reformers within the Church from time to time reverted. These reversions were nearly always short-lived, for the plain reason that they affected to ignore some of the most potent and paramount of human instincts—the craving for power and for wealth as an instrument of power and luxury. The development of Christian doctrines and the ritual of the Roman Church moved, as we have seen, unerringly upon the lines of an economy of power, and the skilful use of doctrine for enlarging the material resources of the Church grew into a fine art of practical psychology.

Neither in England nor in continental countries do any closely reliable measures of the acquired wealth of the Church exist. But all authorities agree that towards the close of the Middle Ages a very large proportion of the land-values was concentrated in its hands, at a time when agriculture was in every country the dominant factor in the economic system. Hallam, writing of the close of the period, says : [1] " The enormous and in a large measure ill-gotten opulence of the regular clergy had long since excited jealousy in every part of Europe." " A larger proportion of landed wealth was constantly accumulating in hands which lost nothing that they had grasped." Most estimates incline to the view that in this country one-fifth of the occupied land belonged to the

[1] *History of the Middle Ages*, Vol. I, p. 69.

Church, and in Germany, France, Italy, and other good Catholic countries the proportion was probably at least as large. There can be no more convincing testimony to the inroad of Mammon-worship into the Church than the constantly increasing share of property which passed into her hands.

Modern social thinkers, in revolt against the *laissez-faire* competitive individualism of nineteenth-century economic theory and practice, are sometimes prone to refer with favour to the principles which underlay the claims of the medieval Church to regulate industry and commerce in accordance with the organic theory of a sound society. This theory, prescribing equitable rules for economic conduct, subordinating the production of wealth to its vital uses, and regarding the well-being of the community as the paramount consideration in economic activities, can make a specious claim to the sympathy of those who have a keen perception of the disorders of our current economic system.

The theory, indeed, I hold to be essentially sound. Distinctively economic conduct cannot properly be divorced from other lines of conduct, either in individuals or in societies, and should be subject to rational direction applied in the interests of human beings and societies conceived as organic wholes. Such rules, moreover, in order to be applied effectively, should have conscious recognition. The notion that some "invisible hand" or instinctive harmony can take the place of the rational will in regulating any branch of human conduct is a noxious fallacy, the falsehood and folly of which were never more manifest than at the present time. It is, then, fair to recognize that, so far as this central conscious organic purpose underlay the claim of the Catholic Church to regulate economic life, it held a sounder view than that which later on prevailed in modern economic theory and policy. But when we turn from the theory of the Church to its practice, we see how easily incompetence, cowardice, and avarice combined to sterilize its high professions. The moral control claimed by the Church over economic conduct, and embodied in the principle of "justum pretium," or fair dealing, was everywhere subjected to compromise and concessions which ate away its ethics, and made it servile to the interests of the richer members of the community. It did little at any time to curb the greed and rapacity of the strong. Partly by reason of the vague idealism of its principles, which rendered them inapplicable in their simplicity to the complex affairs of business life, but largely from an insufficient faith in their application, the Church failed of fulfilment. Thus **Mammon,** carrying on a constant guerilla warfare against the spiritual rule, reduced its supremacy to impotence. But still more signal was Mammon's victory within the bosom of the Church itself, inspiring it to the discovery and cultivation of doctrines and rites which became ever finer instruments for the acquisition of wealth, and for the subordination of spiritual to worldly goods.

Chapter III

Protestantism and Business

I

THE sixteenth century was an age of new and stirring adventure in many fields of human activity. The mariner's compass had given a freedom of the seas to adventurous traders. The discovery of the Cape route to India and of the American continent had destroyed the trading and maritime supremacy of the Italian cities. First Spain and Portugal, later England and Holland, established commercial relations along the African and American coasts and with the islands of the Pacific. Europe, hitherto stinted in the precious metals, which flowed to the East in payment for spices and other Eastern luxuries, was now nourished financially with gold and silver from the American mines. Spanish treasure-ships bearing the plunder of Mexico and Peru became the prey of British or Dutch pirates, much as the rum-runners and bootleggers in America to-day are prey of the highjackers and the racketeers.

This new flow of the precious metals played into the hands of early capitalism, both on its financial and industrial sides. It brought the development of a money-market, with the financing not only of great foreign trading companies, but also of new mining and textile trades. In England the ruin of the old feudal aristocracy in the Wars of the Roses and the passage of the Church lands into the hands of new business men were transforming the old routine of feudal custom, and industrializing large sections of rural England. These distinctively economic changes coincided with the great new revival and expansion of learning, literary, artistic, scientific, known as the Renaissance. The flood of fresh thought and speculation which burst first in Italy, and then flowed north and west, was not merely a revelation of the art and literature of Hellas. It was a new free stir in the mind of educated man throughout Europe, exhibiting itself in scepticism and revolt against dogmas and accepted standards, religious, scientific, political, and ethical. The mingled rationalism and imaginative enterprise of this spiritual revival come home best to us in the literature and the adventure of the Elizabethan days. It was a sense of liberty in the world of thought and matter, on every plane of activity; new worlds to conquer and the stirring of a free spirit for the task of conquest.

The urges of this new economic and intellectual life were bound to come into conflict with the conservatism and the vested interests, material and moral, of the Catholic Church. The tide of new learning, sweeping through the Universities of Europe from Italy and reaching England first through scholars like Grocyn and Linacre, afterwards raised to the level of enthusiasm by the Dutch visitor Erasmus and his disciples More and Colet, was not with any clear intent an attack upon orthodox religion. But none the less it carried the seeds of a Protestant revolt. A definite anti-clericalism already lay slumbering in the growing resentment against the powers, privileges, and possessions of the Church, before any plain doctrinal divergences were manifested. The combination of a revived Lollardry and Bible-reading and the new learning among the growing lay educated class undoubtedly helped Henry VIII in his substitution of clerical nationalism for the rule of Rome. The printing press was the most revolutionary weapon ever placed in the hands of man. It enabled him to test the authority of the Church and to put his own judgment on the evidences of his faith.

This brief survey of leading influences and events may help us in considering how far economic forces produced or moulded Protestantism and its Puritan distillation. The Roman Church, as a Catholic institution autocratically overriding the new institution of the national state, claiming both spiritual and temporal supremacy, and a supremacy enforced by innumerable economic suckers, aroused deep hostility among the self-respecting burghers of the growing cities of Germany, Holland, and England. Not the doctrines or the rites of the Church, but the exactions and restrictions it imposed were the roots of this discontent. In this sense and to this extent the causes of Protestantism may be said to have been economic. The central and local parasitism by which a large proportion of the product of the industry of the people passed to the support of local monasteries, chantries, and churches, and through them, or directly, to swell the papal treasury, was felt as a growing grievance even among the religious-minded laity. The new nationalism of the Tudors, with their centralized state government, intensified these usurpations of a foreign master, and greatly aided Henry in his schemes of monarchical aggrandisement. In one quite definite way the plunder of the monasteries and abbeys helped the cause of Protestantism. "That unhallowed booty," writes Disraeli, "created a factitious aristocracy, ever fearful lest they might be called upon to disgorge their sacrilegious spoil. To prevent this they took refuge in political religionism, and paltering with the disturbed consciences or the pious fantasies of a portion of the people, organised them into religious sects. These became the unconscious Pretorians of their ill-gotten domains. At the head of these religionists, they have continued ever since to govern, or powerfully to influence, this country." [1]

Though there is an element of fantastic exaggeration in this imputation of continuous Whig politics to the new Tudor gentry, the dispersion of Church lands undoubtedly helped to build up a solid country block which co-operated with the new bourgeoisie against every attempt to restore Catholicism during the sixteenth and seventeenth centuries. Most of the purchasers of the Church lands probably remained faithful adherents of the Church of England, but a not inconsiderable number of their descendants in the Stuart days were found among the Independents and other sectaries that furnished Cromwell's armies with men and funds.

It would also be true to say that in England, as also in the continental countries subject to the new commercial and financial influences and opportunities, the constant drainage of wealth passing to the Roman Church was felt as a grave impediment to economic progress. Moreover, the diversion of this wealth from the care of the poor and other charitable uses to the support of idle, luxurious, and evil-living monks and clerics was a growing scandal in all Catholic countries, and especially in Rome itself, where it was associated with a widespread disbelief in the basic doctrines of Christianity and the reduction of religion to a profitable formalism.

It is no wonder that pious pilgrims to Rome from other Catholic lands were shocked by what they saw and heard, and that their reports on their return helped to feed the anticlericalism of countries like Germany, the Netherlands, Scandinavia, and Britain. Genuine moral disapproval thus came to be blended with economic discontents. "Loose from Rome" meant a sounder religion, national or local in its

[1] *Coningsby*, Bk. II, ch. 1.

organization, and with full control of its own resources and offices.

* * *

The Protestant churches, however, were not in their first intent disposed to relax any of the spiritual authority exercised by organized religion over the moral and economic conduct of their members. It is not true to represent the new sectarian teaching of Lutherans, Calvinists, Independents, as the substitution of the authority of the Book for that of the Church, and of the private judgment of the individual for priestly authority. Though the Bible, now translated, was made accessible to the minority who were capable of reading, the authority of the reformed Church of England was never based, and is not now based, upon the authority of the Bible, but upon the continuous inspiration of the Church : the right of private judgment is in all matters of faith and doctrine subject to the authority of that Church. Nor was there in this matter any substantial difference in the attitude of the Protestant churches. Their founders and early spiritual leaders claimed for their several Churches an authority of doctrinal interpretation and of moral regimen as real as, and in the case of Calvinism more rigorous than, that exercised by the Roman Church.

Luther's intention and personal influence were not directed to release the economic or business conduct of men from the rule of spiritual life exercised by the Christian community. His earlier attitude during his reforming activities was a disparagement of material gain, an indifference towards the economic life. " The pursuit of material gain beyond personal needs must thus appear as a symptom of lack of grace, and since it can apparently only be attained at the expense of others, directly reprehensible." [1] His later views led him to value more highly the work of the world. It was the familiar attitude of spiritual conservatives. Divine Providence had placed men in their proper " calling," and it was their duty to adapt themselves to this appointed " station in life." The early Lutheran Church, thus inspired, cannot be regarded as friendly to capitalism. Luther's own repudiation of usury, or indeed interest of any kind, involves a definitely reactionary attitude towards the rising commercial and financial capitalism of his time.

Mr. Tawney makes the following interesting comments upon the position taken, not only by the Lutherans, but also by other important Protestant sects : " If it is true that the

[1] Max Weber, *The Protestant Ethic*, p. 84.

Reformation released forces which were to act as a solvent of the traditional attitude of religious thought to social and economic issues, it did so without design, and against the intention of most reformers." " In the sixteenth century religious teachers of all shades of opinion still searched the Bible, the Fathers, and the *corpus juris canonici* for light on practical questions of social morality, and as far as the first generation of reformers was concerned, there was no intention, among either Lutherans, or Calvinists, or Anglicans, of relaxing the rules of good conduct which were supposed to control economic transactions and social relations. If anything, their tendency was to interpret them with a more rigorous severity, as a protest against the moral laxity of the Renaissance, and in particular, against the avarice which was thought to be peculiarly the sin of Rome." [1]

Thus, in estimating the influence of Protestantism upon economic theory and conduct, we must distinguish the intention of the Reformers from what may be termed the natural consequences of their reforms, and the precepts of the early enthusiasts of reform from the practices of the succeeding generations of their adherents. The early reformers did not abandon the idea of a Church-civilization in which all departments of individual and social conduct should be regulated in acordance with the law of God, as interpreted and administered by the Church.

The severance of " business " from the moral control of the Christian community, and the adoption of a *laissez-faire* individualism had no place whatever in early Protestantism. How the severance was actually achieved, how the Protestant virtues and valuations became the nutriment of capitalistic energy and enterprise, is best studied in Calvinism and the sects which its teaching inspired.

Calvinism was characterized by its spiritual isolationism. A man's communication with his God was not through the organization of his Church, important as that was to his religious life, but a directly personal one. And yet, as numberless records indicate, Church discipline was remorselessly imposed upon every branch of personal and social conduct. Calvinism, alike in the country of its origin, Switzerland, and in those of its early penetration, Holland, Scotland, France, England, and later America, was brought into close contact with the changes of a bustling urban life. Luther's economic attitude remained that of a countryman. But Geneva, Antwerp, Amsterdam, London, and Edinburgh were filled

[1] *Religion and the Rise of Capitalism*, pp. 84–5.

with men occupied with industry, commerce, and finance. Did Calvinism take hold in these countries because of the more independent and self-reliant stock that were born in or gravitated to these centres of progressive business? Was it the religion that suited this type of men in this economic environment, a process of natural selection? Or did the Calvinist faith, with its unflinching logic, its lack of emotionalism, its severe rules of personal ethics, supply the forces and conditions of success in the new competitive system that was everywhere beginning to displace the narrowly ordered customary processes of guild life? Mr. Tawney goes so far as to assert that "it is perhaps the first systematic body of religious teaching which can be said to recognize and applaud the economic virtues."[1]

A society of hard, thoughtful, industrious men and women, bent upon their personal salvation, to be achieved, under Divine predestination, by conduct conducive to the glory of God, was easily led to regard its occupations and "callings" as chief instruments in the spiritual life thus conceived. Every business activity, not expressly sinful, was regarded by them as conducive to the glory of God. The qualities that made for business success in the new economic order were qualities valued on their own account as contributory to a godly life, and the regulations of their churches gave them the social approval.

What, then, were these useful economic qualities? Some were positive—viz., industry, initiative and enterprise, honesty, foresight, calculation. Others were negative, the ascetic virtues of temperance and continence, the avoidance of pleasures and amusements; thrift and accumulation of capital. Now, as we shall observe, this way of life was more or less common to all Protestant sects, at any rate in their early stages. But Calvinism was peculiarly adapted to their encouragement and effective practice. It did not keep the mind concentrated upon the next world to the neglect of this. It eschewed "enthusiasm," a disturbing emotionalism hostile to sound business enterprise and orderly work. Its doctrine of predestination relieved the saint of the brooding anxiety of spirit which was apt to sap the energy otherwise available for money-making. Above all, disregarding the express teaching of Christ about the dangers of riches, it regarded them with favour as the natural fruit of business ingenuity and toil, condemning only their misuse for self-indulgence and ostentation. Mammon, in fact, was taken into the service of God

[1] *Op. cit.*, p. 105.

C

as a junior partner. This crude way of putting it was not, indeed, distinctly incorporated in the Calvinistic theology, but it emerged in their practical ethics of life. " God has been very good to me," was the naïve comment of a modern English business man of high political status when reflecting on the wealth which successful practice of the economic virtues placed at his disposal.

Rationalism may at first sight seem a curious term to apply to Calvinism. And yet, given certain assumptions, it helps greatly to explain the close pact between God and Mammon, success in this world contributing to salvation in the next, which marked not only strict Calvinism as it appeared in Geneva and Scotland, but in different degrees all the leading nonconformist bodies from the sixteenth century onward.

The doctrine of Predestination was a dogmatic background of all the sects that came under the Calvinist influence. It was not only the principle of Presbyterianism in Britain and in North America. It was incorporated in the Independent Savoy Declaration of 1658, the Baptist Confession of 1689, and found a place in the early Wesleyan movement under the teaching of its most important thinker Whitefield.[1]

The ascetic Protestantism of the Calvinist doctrine nourished industrialism at the very time when it most required this moral nutriment. For the growing organization of commerce and finance, and the beginnings of machine production in the manufactures, formed a large demand for capital, the fruit of saving. Honest industry, accompanied by abstemious living, necessarily bred a surplus income which could be used for the enlargement and improvement of the business that furnished it, or could be employed in some outside loan or investment. Predestination might, indeed, have led to a fatalism that would have atrophied business enterprise, had it been a subject for emotional brooding, or it might have separated the elect from the outside world and led to a monastic community life. That these results did not occur is attributed by most students of pietism to what they term " the ethic of the calling," the realization of salvation within the everyday routine of this life as a preparation for the next. But a consideration of the typical mentality of the urban Swiss, Dutch, Scots, or Huguenots will lead us to impute a large measure of economic determinism in the application of their creed. The material and social environment of these peoples, moulding their stock and character, evoked a sturdy, self-reliant, energetic type which needed to express itself in the activities of everyday life.

[1] Weber, *op. cit.*, p. 125.

These peoples found in Calvinism a spiritual stiffening that was highly serviceable to this daily conduct. Though the religion they adopted set no formal value upon worldly success and the accumulation of worldly goods, by an easy " rationalization " the wealth which was the natural fruit of industrious application to " a calling " became a testimony to a good life. " The doctrine that inward salvation should be expressed in continuous labour merged with the belief that success was the hall-mark of godliness." [1] Insensibly the religious bourgeois of this type accepted the current rules of honesty and legality in a business world that had already broken away from the shackles of scholasticism and its Canon Law. Capital and credit, the guiding factors in modern business, were detached from the obsolete conceptions of avarice and usury, and competition between presumed equals was regarded as the natural method of determining " a fair price." " Capital and credit are indispensable; the financier is not a parasite, but a useful member of society; and lending at interest, provided that the rate is reasonable, and that loans are made freely to the poor, is not *per se* more extortionate than any other of the economic transactions without which human affairs cannot be carried on." [2]

Given this acceptance of a " calling," the adoption of ordinary business-bargaining as the method of determining a price, the distinction between business loans, or investment, and " usury," and a long stride in the direction of *laissez-faire* capitalism had been made. You were not to oppress your workmen, or otherwise to " grind the faces of the poor," or to take an unfair advantage in a market by " engrossing," " forestalling," or other forms of monopoly. But wealth made by honest industry, skill, and enterprise, was in a sense God's reward in this world, something " added unto you." If you like, you can interpret all this as a compromise, imposed upon the original pattern of Calvinism by the pressure of business interests in the commercial centres where Calvinist doctrine and discipline were first planted. The ordinary conduct of life as practised by a Calvinist (or indeed by any of the ascetic sects of Protestantism), enabled him to thrive and to accumulate this world's goods. The abandonment of the old Church canons for industry and commerce, now rendered obsolete in all the advanced countries of Europe, led to a sharper distinction between the origins or modes of acquiring wealth

---

[1] Margaret James, *Social Problems and Poverty during the Puritan Revolution*, p. 18.
[2] Tawney, p. 108.

and the uses made of acquired wealth. The continuous tendency was towards a loosening of the restrictions of business conduct even among " the elect." Church government and its " godly discipline " in the reign of English Puritanism came to concern itself less and less with the modes of getting wealth, more and more with the modes of spending and misspending it. The preacher before the Lord Mayor and Aldermen in 1655 enunciates the doctrine that " Wisdom is good without an inheritance, but it cannot doe so much good when it is seated in a poor man as when it is joyned with an inheritance." [1] Though Baxter and a few other preachers and teachers sought to formulate rules of fair trading in conformity with the old traditions, these were regarded for the most part as obstructive to modern industry and commerce. They were treated in the same way in which the maxims of the Sermon on the Mount have always been treated in the Western world. They were admired and even recognized as noble ideals, but were disregarded in practice.

It must be remembered that up to this time very few men in this country had ventured to question the principle and rights of private property or the equitable distribution of income. There had, indeed, been a scattering of Antinomians, Anabaptists, and Millenarians, who, while differing in their religious positions, agreed in teaching that the land should be accessible to all, and that there should be a community of goods. During the Puritan Revolution the extreme doctrine of these sects influenced the agrarian movement led by Winstanley, and the brief-lived Digger agitation aimed at establishing a vague sort of social democracy under the Commonwealth. " At this very day," says Winstanley, " poor people are forced to work for a miserable wage which is not sufficient to provide them with bread, while those who dwell in idleness enjoy the fulness of the earth." " But I tell you and your Preachers Scripture which says the poor shall inherit the earth is really and materially to be fulfilled." [2]

But the solid control of the Puritan Revolution lay in the hands of the prosperous and powerful middle-class, who desired nothing less than close scrutiny into origins of wealth and the business relations of rich and poor. Oppressive landlords who enclose lands or evict tenants without consideration of their vital interests are indeed condemned by " the best people," but the idea of questioning the right of owning land and of charging rents for its tenancy seldom entered the minds of Christian moralists. As business grew up on a large scale,

[1] Margaret James, p. 18.   [2] *Idem*, p. 340.

its profits and the interest on money invested in it were accepted as equally natural with rent. In both cases legal right should be qualified by consideration of hard cases. Extortion was hostile to the sense of fair play (always the basic principle of English morality) and was pilloried by Bunyan as a sin " most commonly committed by men of trade, who without all conscience, when they have an advantage will make a prey of their neighbour."

But, with the elaboration and expansion of markets for goods and services, " selling too dear " or " buying too cheap " became less and less possible of ascertainment. The " law of supply and demand " acquired more and more a quasi-moral validity as indicative of equal benefit to the two parties. The Puritans attempted, indeed, in their earlier Church communities to lay down and to enforce discipline in the detailed conduct of a business life. But neither the temper of their adherents nor the new commercial environment of their time favoured such attempts. For " Puritanism was strongest among those classes who were best able to take care of themselves and had nothing to gain and all to lose by the interference of Church and State in economic affairs." [1]

II

The acquisitive and the possessive urges are in peaceful times the commonest and most persistent forms of that " will to power," that sense of personal importance, which is the subtlest and most multiform spirit in man. In many people it is accompanied by an equally intense urge towards conspicuous expenditure and extravagant luxury. But in every community there are orderly and timid souls, with no hankering after enjoyment or display. These find their satisfaction in putting their earnings into a stocking, or, in less primitive conditions, into a savings bank, or, when these savings are of a large amount, investing them in gilt-edged securities. As speculative enterprise offers great business opportunities, a third form of economic spirit displays itself—the zest for the activities and hazards of the business life itself, the lust for power in its most modern form. It is this last that characterizes modern capitalism and furnishes its controlling personal influences. The spendthrift, the miser, the speculator, are the extremes of these attitudes towards money. Perhaps in fairness we should add a fourth, the generous public spirit

[1] James, p. 16.

which not infrequently emerges in a successful money-maker and leads him to find his satisfaction in liberal expenditure on educational, hygienic, or other public benefits. Indeed, there is a modern tendency for the public to expect of a successful business man large contributions to charitable causes. This expectation easily fuses with a recognition that liberal donations act as a protective covering for high-handed and unscrupulous business methods. Religion still has a considerable share in these benefactions, and the social ethics of the pulpit are seldom devoted to close scrutiny of money-making processes, or to denunciation of the deceitfulness of riches.

But, returning to our four-fold differentiation of monetary conduct as a "will to power," the Puritan churches have always condemned spendthrifts and luxurious living. Timid thrift, the careful nursing of a nest-egg, is the conduct prescribed for the industrious worker who is a church member. Large capital for profitable business enterprise and the employment of industrious workers is regarded as an instrument of grace. Public benefactions are the fruits of grace.

Thus, in their attitude towards both productive processes and expenditure, the Puritan churches favoured the rise of a prosperous bourgeoisie, the makers and owners of a continuously increasing proportion of the national wealth. Their early restraints upon the conduct of business, soon found to be incompatible with joint-stock capitalism in industry, trade, and finance, tended to break down, while a competitive *laissez-faire* system, based on individual rational utilitarianism, received the tacit sanction and implied approval of the churches. Though the first reformers were largely drawn from the middle classes, either of the townsmen or the peasantry, as time went on most members of the reformed churches were manual workers, in large part hired labourers. The religious appeal was not the same for them as for their masters. Their lot or calling required obedience to (divinely appointed !) masters, routine industry under proper discipline, contentment with their wages and other conditions of work, abstinence from drink and other dissipations and amusements. In these different ways capitalism was aided by the ascetic Puritanism of the seventeenth and eighteenth centuries, the traces of which remain to-day in the more serious remnants of Protestantism.

III

So far we have dwelt mainly upon the Calvinist creed and temper, as manifested in the reformed churches, in their bearing upon business and the economic side of human life. But Calvinism had not a monopoly of economic discipline and asceticism. Whether the salvation of the individual soul was to be achieved by God's arbitrary will, man's faith, or his good works, or by some curious blend of the three, a strict discipline of life was usually enjoined upon each individual, including strict rules of economic behaviour. Perhaps the most thoroughgoing exponent of this discipline was Richard Baxter in his *Christian Directory, or a Summa of Practical Theologie and Cases of Conscience.* Here economic conduct is treated as subordinate to the rules of Christian ethics. Whether the law of the land permits or not, the Christian is bound by the golden rule and a right regard for the public good in all his business transactions.

The Christian " must not only eschew the obvious extortions practised by the monopolist, the engrosser, the organizer of a corner or a combine. He must carry on his business in the spirit of one who is conducting a public service; he must order it for the advantage of his neighbour as much as, and if his neighbour be poor, more than his own." So Mr. Tawney expresses the spirit of Baxter's teaching, and Bunyan, writing a few years later his *Life and Death of Mr. Badman,* enunciates the same principles. Within the fold of Protestantism arose several such attempts to revert to what was held to be plain gospel teaching and to urge its application to modern economic conduct. The failure of these efforts of what may properly be called Christian Socialism, alike in its business ethics and its asceticism, is the most interesting exhibition of the power of Mammon to win to his purposes the devotees of a saintly life. The fuller exploration of this failure is, however, best deferred until we have traced the same process of spiritual struggle and collapse in other churches.

Wesleyanism, through the teaching of its founder, takes higher ground as an economic doctrine than any of the earlier Protestant sects. For though to it, as to them, the individual life and character were the instruments of spiritual progress, the moral perfectibility which was the centre of Wesley's creed was not limited merely, or perhaps mainly, to the end of personal salvation in another world. The perfection of the individual was a basis for a system of social ethics.[1] "Above all," the new enthusiasts were warned, " do not make the care of future things a pretence for neglecting present duty." [2]

The commendation of the industrial virtues by Wesley was especially addressed to the workers who formed the main body of his early followers. On the productive side of the economic life they must be industrious, for "without industry we are neither fit for this life, nor for the world to come." [3] On the consuming side they were to live a life of seriousness and abstinence.

" We do not find any other body of people who abstain from fashionable diversions, from reading plays, romances, or books of humour, from singing innocent songs, or talking in a merry, gay, diverting manner ; your plainness of dress ; your manner of dealing in trade ; your exactness in observing the Lord's day ; your scrupulosity as to things that have not paid custom ; your total abstinence from spirituous liquors (unless in cases of necessity)." [4]

The relation between employer and employee was treated by Wesley in terms of paternalism. Employers were in some sense responsible for the bodies as well as the souls of those placed under their charge. On the question of wages no consistent policy is discernible. Wesley was not only in favour of fair prices, but on one occasion commended " mob " action to coerce " forestallers " who bought up corn to starve the poor.[5] But evidently he had no principle whereby to define either " fair prices " or " fair wages," and we find him thus advising a member of his church : " To servants I would give full as much as others give for the same service ; and not more." This, of course, accepts the dubious assumption that the current wage is, in fact, fair and sufficient. But, generally speaking, we are told, " Wesley and his associates thought in terms of personal responsibility, fair prices, and fair wages, in a day when those conceptions were rapidly losing all of their meaning." [6] So the theoretic view of a divinely sanctioned calling, either for employer or worker, had no real relation to the new capitalist industry.

As for the use of riches, Wesley took the line of " steward-ship " and " trust." God's purpose was to be the guide. " As to yourself," wrote Wesley to a man of property, " you are not the proprietor of any thing ; no, not of one shilling in the

---

[1] W. J. Warner, *The Wesleyan Movement*, p. 71.
[2] Wesley, *Works*, Vol. V, p. 390.   [3] Warner, p. 141.
[4] Wesley, *Works*, Vol. VII, p. 123.
[5] Warner, p. 150.   [6] *Idem*, p. 151.

world. You are only the steward of what another entrusts you with, to be laid out, not according to your will but his. . . . Is not God the sole proprietor of all things ? " [1] But who was to interpret the terms of this stewardship ? Certain kinds of expenditure were evidently right. You must first pay your debts. One must " owe no man anything." Next, you must provide for the necessities of your vocation. " Men in business are to lay up as much as necessary for the carrying on " (and expansion ?) " of that business." Next comes the claims for the " reasonable wants " of oneself and one's dependents, including such provision for one's survivors " as would keep them above want." If your business yields a surplus beyond such provisions, it shall go " to satisfy the needs of the community "—*i.e.*, to charity.

From the first it was recognized by the Wesleyans that a moral and godly life would contribute to material success. Thus it was an obvious deduction that such success should be regarded as a mark of Divine approval. A natural corollary of this view was that poverty was due to moral and religious defects. But this moral individualism was a later product in Wesleyanism. Wesley himself denounced it. " That common objection, they are poor only because they are idle is wickedly, devilishly false." [2] To him the central cause of poverty lay in inequitable consumption, luxurious living for the few, the denial of necessaries for the many. The due provision of employment at reasonable pay for all was then as now the economic crux. Wesley, no more than Church Congresses of to-day, had a solution.

How far the individual is responsible for success or failure in his " calling," whether as business man or worker, is a question perhaps incapable of exact answer. That personal qualities and activities are the direct determinants of how much work a man does, and the quantity and quality of its product, is indisputable. But that same product may vary indefinitely, as to its value or market price, according to the general state of trade—*i.e.*, the quantity and quality of all sorts of other goods which exchange against this product in the processes of the market. Now one industrious man cannot have any power to affect this " demand " for his product, though the real wage he gets for it depends upon it. The failure to recognize this fundamental truth that " value," and therefore " wages," are for the most part socially and not individually determined, is certain to obfuscate the minds of all who concentrate upon the character and habits of individual

[1] Warner, p. 155.   [2] *Journal*, Vol. IV, p. 52.

workers. The later Wesleyans, like other religionists, fell into this error, though their founder had a clearer understanding of the nature of poverty. This was, indeed, only to be expected. For it soon came to pass that employers, not themselves associated with Methodism, learned to recognize the advantage of employing in posts of responsibility, as foremen and over-lookers, sober, industrious members of the Methodist local churches. These foremen in their turn would bring into the works labourers whom they knew to be sober and industrious. For the reformation of the most dissolute members of the industrial towns and the mining villages by Methodism became common knowledge. The early persecution and prejudice against this " canting sect " and its " revival " methods gave way before a growing recognition of these serviceable fruits, so that in many quarters by no means friendly to the new church, Methodists got a good name for domestic as well as for industrial service.

When the undoubted success of Wesleyans in business is taken into account, it must not be forgotten that the rise and progress of their sect coincided with the period of the eighteenth and early nineteenth centuries commonly styled the Industrial Revolution. This rapid transformation of industry by the new machinery and power afforded great opportunities to men possessed of the economic virtues. " We find also thousands of young men," said a prominent Methodist at the end of the eighteenth century, " who, by virtue and temperance, by industry and economy, by happy connections and the blessing of God on their labours, have risen from labour to affluence, and now fill the leading situations in commercial life. . . . Happiness and smiling plenty have been diffused through the towns and villages in which their manufactures have suc-ceeded." [1] So clear, indeed, was the connection between personal steadiness and business success that it helped largely to recruit members to a Society which " made good " in both worlds. The early Wesleyans, buoyed up by enthusiasm, kept their virtue amid the temptations of the world. As business prospered, they were distinguished by devotion to public and private charities. They even gave up some opportunities of gain that conflicted with their principles, refusing as shop-keepers to desecrate the Sabbath, abstaining from the profit-able practice of smuggling, and, as innkeepers, discouraging excess in drinking. But as the early enthusiasm waned and Wesleyanism became a family tradition, this restrictive austerity weakened. " Then the temptation to dilute the

[1] Joseph Sutcliffe, *A Review of Methodism*, cited Warner, p. 191.

moral imperative of the divine-ownership theory, which ordered the disposition of all money above the bare needs of the individual for the good of the community, became acute. Wesley and the early Methodists were felt to be too radical. . . . Therefore a rising group of prosperous Methodists repudiated this part of the teaching by the apparently innocuous judgment that in this respect Wesley was simply impracticable." [1]

Thus the economic by-products of godliness, alike on the side of industry and consumption, were more and more diluted by Mammonism, until all that remained was a certain mood and habit of philanthropy.

We have seen that in Wesleyanism, as indeed among Baptists and other reforming sects, a double interacting process takes place favourable to business success. Persons are attracted to these religious tenets whose lives are less occupied than those of their fellows with the pleasures and dissipations of society, and whose seriousness of mind is expressed in habits of forethought and responsibility. These propensities in their turn are nourished and strengthened by the godly life of a compact religious community, and are directed usefully to business ends by the sense of a " vocation." Both on the side of production and of consumption this careful austerity strengthens their economic position. In a word, they make money, and are sparing in expenditure. They might, of course, spend all their surplus in charity, but in practice they put most of it as " savings " back into their business. This thrift was particularly " blessed " at a time when the new factory system and the expanding home and foreign markets required large new supplies of capital.

There is, however, another social factor which operates towards business success—namely, the collective and mutual self-help among the local members of a sect who are able to trust one another and willing to deal with one another on preferential terms. Nor is this advantage confined to the local units of such sects. Leading church members, usually of responsibility and means, become personally known to one another, by conferences and other gatherings, so that the spiritual union of such a church easily improvises useful business bonds. The economic value of a reliable integrity of character has been utilized by all the minor sects.

The Quakers in some ways present a unique example of a working alliance between God and Mammon in which Mammon has been less successful than elsewhere in establishing supremacy. This is partly attributable to the clearer consciousness

[1] Warner, p. 147.

of social and economic maladies in the founders of the Society of Friends, and the larger part assigned to the redress of such grievances in the " concerns " of the Society. Originating in the same ferment of religious, political, and social thought and emotion that marked the mid-seventeenth century, Quakerism stood out from the larger groupings of Independents, Baptists, etc., by the nature of its challenge to the accepted thought and practice of the time. It was distinguished in two ways. The principle of guidance by the Inner Light in all branches of human conduct, while it differed essentially from the authoritative attitude assumed by the Calvinist churches, did not land the Friends in the quandary of reliance on a Book whose inapplicability to many modern problems has been so evident as to evoke an art of spiritual casuistry. Nor was the individual judgment the supreme arbiter of right and wrong. For the Inner Light was the inspiring and directing presence in each person as a member of a spiritual community. In this sense it was a collective guidance, giving rules of conduct suitable for general acceptance. The Meetings were occasions for sharing with one another the light which came to each soul in regard to every activity of secular life.

Still more significant for our purpose was the close attention given by George Fox and other early teachers to the ethics of business life, alike on the side of industry and of consumption. Fox, as a disturber of the existing social economy, was nearer to the Levellers, Diggers, and other social-democratic agitators who formed the left wing of the Puritan movement during the mid-century. " It is significant," writes Miss James, " that Quakerism appealed to the lowest classes more than any other variety of Puritanism," and one writer went so far as to complain that " it was made up of the dregs of the people." [1] Fox preached Democracy in its full sense of liberty, equality, and fraternity, attacking the abuses of property and exposing ruthlessly the causes of poverty. Though the wage-problem did not figure prominently in his gospel, he was deeply concerned with the relief of poverty and its attendant ills. " The Quaker plea for simplicity in dress and for restraint in all forms of recreation was not merely an ascetic trait, or a Puritan survival, but was based by George Fox on the principle of the common brotherhood of man. It was a practical way of trying to advance the more equal distribution of wealth." [2]

It cannot, however, be said that any of the early exponents of Quakerism penetrated deeply into the economic problems

[1] *Op. cit.*, p. 19.
[2] Isabel Grubb, *Quakerism and Industry before* 1800, p. 24.

of poverty and the distribution of wealth, though they, like Wesley, protested vigorously against " forestalling " and " engrossing " and other oppressive practices. On methods of trade they held that the " Inner Light " would enable a trader to discern the " fair value " of what he sold.

Except so far as a well-grounded reputation for truth, honesty, and industry is serviceable for the business life, there is no ground for holding that Quakerism in its early days was an advantageous qualification for money-making. Fines, distraints, and imprisonment were serious bars to worldly success. Moreover, scruples regarding the undertaking of luxury trades or the bestowal of labour on decorative processes seriously interfered with the earning power of many Friends. When Gilbert Labey, a leading tailor in London during the Commonwealth, became a Friend, " he gave up the making of fashionable garments and confined his work to the plain apparel which he thought consistent with Christian simplicity." In 1676 and 1677 the " National Meeting " took up the matter, and pronounced against " making and selling . . . things which truth will not allow of . . . such they deemed to be the merchandise of gold and silver lace, gaudy ribbons, silks, etc., all which kind of traffic several persons who had been concerned in, when they came to be of this judgment, did lay down for conscience sake." [1]

As time went on and Friends acquired a considerable place in shipping, banking, the iron and steel and other thriving trades, a good deal of laxity seems to have crept in. In 1693 the London Yearly Meeting issued a protest against professing Quakers " carrying guns in their ships, supposing thereby to defend and secure themselves and their ships, contrary to their former principle and practice." [2] Others seem to have engaged in fitting out privateers, or in financing them. Perhaps the most typical case was that of iron-masters engaging in the manufacture of arms, which came up on various occasions during the wars of the eighteenth century.

The part taken by Quakers in the anti-slavery movement has been a conspicuous testimony to their sense of human equality. And yet it seems strange how slow the movement was towards practical achievement. It was in 1675 that a companion of George Fox, William Edmundson, after visiting the Barbadoes, delivered a remonstrance to Friends in Maryland and Virginia against slave-holding. From that time on sporadic protests were made in Pennsylvania against " the buying and keeping of negroes " and against " bringing in any

---

[1] Isabel Grubb, *op. cit.*, pp. 94–5.   [2] *Op. cit.*, p. 128.

more negroes." But "the Society gave these memorials a cold reception. The love of gain and power was too strong on the part of the wealthy and influential planters and merchants, who had become slave-holders, to allow the scruples of the Chester Meeting to take the shape of discipline." So also in New England nothing was done to interfere with this lucrative trade until 1727, when the practice of importing negroes was condemned. "That the practice was continued, notwithstanding, for many years afterwards, is certain." [1] Not until John Woolman had devoted the latter part of his life (from 1742 to 1762) to a crusade against slave-dealing and slave-owning was the Society solidly converted to the cause of abolition, and in Virginia, where slavery had its strongest hold, as late as 1784 offenders against the manumission recommendation of 1773 were formally expelled from the Society. Woolman's general views upon wealth and poverty may be taken as representative of the earlier Quaker teaching : " It is equitable that some should have greater possessions than others, so long as they use them faithfully for the good of all." In other words, equity was applied less to origins of wealth than to the uses to which it was put—the familiar " stewardship " or " trust " theory of economic obligations.

The Quaker connexion with banking, which Cobbett assailed so virulently, was due not merely to the saving propensity of Friends, but to their early occupation in the two great English industries of the seventeenth century, farming and weaving. Both industries, as then conducted, needed temporary advances of money, and the Quakers, being trusted by all, lent their spare cash and so became bankers.[2] Caution, accuracy in detail, shrewdness in judging character, and a facility of forecast, qualities possessed by Friends in common with the Jews,[3] were of special value in the banking industry.

---

[1] *The Journal of John Woolman.* Intr. pp. 8, 9.

[2] " Two of the largest banking combines in England at the present day are of Quaker origin, and have absorbed into themselves tens of private banks founded by other Quakers."—Isabel Grubb, p. 165.

[3] How far the important part played by the Jews in modern capitalism, especially upon its commercial and financial side, is directly traceable to their religion may be questioned. But Sombart, in his important work, *The Jews and Modern Capitalism*, contends that the qualities of " rationalism," clear-cut planning and abstract reasoning, together with what he terms their " teleology " (conscious adaptation of means to the end), which distinguish the Jews as religionists, are of prime importance to successful capitalism. These qualities, whether " racial " in a primary sense or only in the secondary sense, as selected for survival in their struggle for life, have enabled them to seize the growing opportunities which a capitalism, ever more impersonal and

From its earliest days Quakerism had been associated with industrial philanthropy. Beginning within the ranks of the Society, schemes were devised for supplying tools and materials to Friends suffering imprisonment. Experience in this work led John Bellers to meet the growing poverty in the early eighteenth century by his " Proposals for raising a College of Industry, of all useful Trades and Husbandry with profit for the rich—a plentiful living for the poor—and a good education for youth, which will be of advantage to the Government by the increase of the people and their riches."

Experiments along the line of this Proposal carried on at workhouses in Clerkenwell, Bristol, and elsewhere, may be regarded as the first practical beginnings in the reform of the degrading administration of our Poor Laws. Though no lasting effects were produced along this line of experiment, they illustrate the wider public interest of Quakers in the economic progress of the workers, so strikingly exhibited in recent times.

In the later eighteenth and early nineteenth centuries, when the modern factory system was growing fast, Quaker firms in the iron and textile trades succeeded better than others in maintaining good personal relations between employers and workers. The beginnings of what are now called Workers' Welfare schemes were laid by Quaker firms in various parts of the country, in the housing of employees, and other conditions of life. Though the new conditions of industry and commerce made the conception of a " just price " more difficult of application than in olden times, the ordinary prevailing theory of *laissez-faire* individualism that substantial justice was obtained by buying at the cheapest price and selling at the dearest, whether the market was in goods or services, was never accepted by " good " Quakers. Some moral obligation both to their employees and to the consumer was recognized, however difficult it might be to define, or to reconcile it with the " law of supply and demand " in the operation of a market.

But, though driven, or induced, to conform in the main operations of industry, commerce, and finance to the ordinary modes of bargaining, Friends have never maintained the

financial in character and ever more international in scope, gives to a people who, scattered through the trading centres of the whole world, maintain common ties of religious and racial unity. There can be no doubt that religion has here been of most material service to successful business enterprises, extending by close intermarriage the bounds of personal confidence so valuable in business undertakings, and cultivating the sense of " God's chosen people " as a fine instrument for money-making.

rigorous distinction which most Christian business men make between Sunday idealism and week-day practice. They have never sought to reconcile the claims of God and Mammon by avowed compromises of the higher claims. This at any rate is true of the faithful adherents of the Society. Spiritual worldlings have always tended to leave the Society and attach themselves to more accommodating churches. As the State and the Municipality in recent times have taken an ever-growing part in the regulation and even the conduct of certain large industrial and other businesses, Quakers have generally given approval and assistance. Not a few of the younger Quakers have adopted the wider socialist attitude, becoming active members of the Labour Party. Others have thrown themselves into policies for setting capitalism upon a more equitable and democratic basis by means of profit-sharing and co-partnership, works committees and pensions schemes. Of perhaps no other religious body can it truthfully be said that the normal tendency of its members is one of constant endeavour to apply to business life and its economic relations principles of justice and humanity directly flowing from the religious creed they hold.

In summarizing the Puritan movement Mr. Tawney writes : " The distinctive note of Puritan teaching was . . . individual responsibility, not social obligation. Training its pupils to the mastery of others through the mastery of self, it prized as a crown of glory the qualities which arm the spiritual athlete for his solitary contest with a hostile world, and dismissed concern with the social order as the prop of weaklings and the Capua of the soul." [1] Creeds holding that each individual soul was an object of separate salvation to be achieved by its own faith, its own works, or by the arbitrary will of God, were disabled by this supreme concern from employing their minds, hearts, and activities for the good of society in this world. They were incapable of translating into effective comradeship the teaching of Christ or of conceiving the ideal of an economic commonwealth in which health, physical comfort and enjoyment, leisure and other good things of this life, may be achieved for mankind. Though efforts to interpret God's will in terms of social service were, as we have seen, occasionally undertaken as belonging to Christian endeavour, the main trend of the Puritan teaching was against them. Even in the Quakers, where this spiritual individualism was merged in the common possession of Divine guidance, there was little disposition to seek such reforms of business structure as to

[1] *Op. cit.*, p. 273.

make the activities of Mammon subject to the teaching of Christ as set forth in his Gospel.

Briefly summarizing the evidence, we may say that the personal mentality and the social environment which brought about the breakaway from the spiritual authority of the Roman Church also made for individualism and capitalist enterprise in the business world. People of a self-reliant, enterprising, rationalist character, fit to achieve success in the new world of economic opportunities that was opening out in the sixteenth, seventeenth, and eighteenth centuries, were drawn by this same character to adopt Protestantism in creed and organization. The moral and religious teaching of most Protestant sects favoured an industrious, honest, orderly, foresighted, ascetic life at a time when these qualities were wanted for the new capitalism.

CHAPTER IV

The Churches and Modern Economic Movements

THIS brief account of the emergence of primitive religious creeds and sentiments from the magic and animism of man's brooding and imaginative mind indicates how an elementary religion, not expressly designed for securing material goods, easily and naturally succumbs to these urgent needs of current human life. For man to wrest a living from the earth, with its ill-known contents and powers of fertility, the irregularity and supreme importance of vegetative and animal fecundity—these matters required all the aid which magic and worship could supply. The magician and the priest must be induced to lend their skilled mysterious help. God, in his most primitive form, must do the work of Mammon : spiritual and physical forces must co-operate in the great economic processes for the maintenance and increase of man. The belief in the power of the religious experts to control the productive forces of nature, and to avert the injurious forces, is early realized as a means of easy living by a priestly caste, the members of which soon learn how to apply to their own material advantage the sacrifices, gifts, or blackmail which experience enables them to appropriate.

Thus from the earliest times a parasitic life is cultivated by priests or priest-kings, accumulating a larger and larger proportion of the current wealth and durable treasures which form the economic surplus in a growing civilization. The higher cults are no exception to this tendency of Mammon to press his claims upon religion. The history of any of the great world religions bears out this tendency. Brahmanism, Buddhism, the religions of Assyria, Babylon, Egypt, are rich with examples of the encroachments of this lust for wealth and economic power upon the spiritual claims and of the ascetic practices which from time to time are expressed in " reform " movements.

Christianity is rightly taken as the chief field for the manifestation of this unending struggle. After the early communism of Christian groups waiting for an immediate Second Coming had evaporated, and from toleration Christianity had advanced to temporal dominion, the Church exercised a double influence in the spheres of industry and property, regulating the first in the supposed interest of Christian ethics, and acquiring larger and larger portions of the second for its own enjoyment and aggrandisement. From time to time, as we see, movements of protest arose within the Church, attempted returns to the ascetic life; but they were either crushed as heresies or sapped by the unconquerable cravings of human nature. The intimate *modus vivendi* established between the Papacy and Mammon during the Middle Ages, and the elaboration of the spiritual tentacles by which the acquisition of property was conducted, seem to the modern mind a miracle of naïve parasitism. The revolt in Britain, Germany, Switzerland, the Netherlands and France against the doctrinal and temporal power of Rome, termed Protestantism, had its special economic significance in two directions. It was a repudiation of the institutional channels through which theocracy was draining the surplus wealth of Catholic countries, fortified in England by the craving of new ambitious men for Church lands. Still more important was the break-up of the restraints upon the new forms of extra-guild industry and trade which formed the beginnings of modern capitalism. This last consideration has led us to identify Protestantism, especially in its nonconformist churches, with the cultivation of a standard of life and morals in which the economic virtues of personal industry and adventure, reasoning, foresight and parsimony, stand out conspicuously.

Our brief examination of certain typical forms of Protestantism shows how difficult it has been to make the new demands of a sound, successful economic life square with the precepts of Christian teaching as expressed in the Gospels. The general tendency was to find a solution of the problem by avoiding close scrutiny into the origins of wealth, and concentrating attention upon the uses to which it should be put. " Make all the money you can by the honest assiduous practice of your ' vocation,' but regard this wealth as a ' trust,' which, after the satisfaction of the reasonable requirements of yourself and your family have been provided for, must be administered charitably for the public good." The general Catholic doctrine and practice of more or less promiscuous charity have, however, been displaced by a more considered policy in interpreting the public good.

This avoidance of economic origins of wealth and adoption

of the " trust " or " stewardship " conception for the employment of surplus wealth constitutes, I think, the prevailing
religious attitude towards economic problems as expressed in
the higher-minded and more public-spirited members of most
Protestant bodies. The established Episcopal Church of this
country has inclined, in its ordinary preaching and teaching,
to renounce all claims to regulate business life in conformity
with Christian principles, as distinct from i..culcating the
ethics of personal integrity and justice. The attachment of
its ministers to the landed interests, from whom its income and
social influence were mainly derived, early made the Church a
bulwark of political and economic conservatism. Until quite
recently, save among a section of the town clergy, there has
been little interest in social-economic problems, except so far
as particular cases were concerned, and little disposition
towards that asceticism which marked the Catholic orders in
their prime, and the Puritan sects almost up to the present
time. The Tractarian movement of the early Victorian era,
and the revivals of Catholic discipline and doctrine within
the Establishment which followed, have brought about new
contacts of the clergy with the labouring classes, especially
in the cities, which have seriously impaired the earlier *modus
vivendi* of God and Mammon. A return to asceticism, partly
as a sympathetic appeal to the personal confidence of the poor
among whom they worked, has been in part also a protest
against the luxuries and extravagances of the rich as indices
of an inequitable apportionment of " this world's goods."
Wherever this sense of protest became conscious, it was the
seed of Christian Socialism. From the mid-nineteenth century a small but growing leaven of this Christian Socialism
has been operative among both the clergy and the lay members
of the Church. It has had bold and eloquent exponents from
the time of Kingsley and Maurice, and the idea of reasserting
for the Church a definite spiritual authority over the organization and ethics of modern business is still entertained by
Christian Socialists in Germany, Austria, Switzerland, and
even in this country. But the ordinary attitude of our
Established Church, as expressed in Congresses or other
authoritative utterances, is one of platitudinarianism, loose,
suave, non-committal, on all important proposals of economic
reform. This is due partly to a genuine disbelief in its
competency to handle economic issues, partly to its feeling of
personal sympathy with the wealthy business classes whose
assistance is more than ever needed to enable it to carry on
the recognized work of a modern parish.

Somewhat different is the present situation in the non-conformist churches. While the earlier asceticism has visibly declined both as a theory and a practice, at any rate among those members who can afford not to be ascetic, there is a widespread concern about the social aspects of business life which is converting large numbers of nonconformist church members into Christian Socialists, or into Socialists *tout purs* if, as is often the case, they fall away from a Christianity which makes no serious attempt to apply Christ's teaching to economic matters.

Here it may be well to consider the influence of the almost sensational collapse of dogmatic beliefs and church attachments here and among the peoples of other civilized countries. Christian Socialism is a pathetic attempt to rally some remnant of belief and moral authority for the churches at a time when the exposure of the falsity or inconsistency of the doctrinal teaching of the Christian churches has conspired with a rapid expansion of new worldly interests, and a scientific spirit related thereto, to bring about the obsolescence of theology. Whether, as in Austria and Bavaria, Christian Socialism is a potent though futile endeavour to restore to the Catholic Church a temporal power which is lost for ever, or, as in England, a new attempt to fuse a spiritual with a mundane motive in the economic reform movement, preserving the union of a morally respectable Mammon and a kindlier and laxer Deity, the procedure is extremely interesting. Whereas on the Continent the break of Socialism with the religion of the churches, Catholic or Protestant, is almost complete, in Britain the spirit of compromise which prevails in every department of conduct has produced a Socialist Party, a large number of whose leaders and adherents are active church members. Few people in this country are definitely " rationalist " in their attitude towards religion, politics, the family, or any other institution. Though utilitarian reasoners in business, we are very slow to apply reason to the assessment of any line of behaviour which carries sentimental or emotional associations. Such minds are still disposed to ascribe separate spheres of rule to God and Mammon. In this they have received much assistance from professional economists. Without subscribing to the crude maxim " Business is Business," these economists limit very severely the sphere of Christian, or any other, ethic in its claims to regulate the economic system. For the economic field is subject to scientific laws which will not bow before ethical considerations. Sir Josiah Stamp, addressing Christian reformers, as a Christian, tells them : " I would say whatever is economically right (*i.e.* inevitable) cannot be morally wrong. For where there is no choice or avoidance there is no moral issue." His argument here is expressly directed to show that the common belief that poverty is due to unjust and alterable distribution of wealth is erroneous. " If the Christian ethic cannot do any better than alter static distribution, it is bankrupt so far as its real effect on economic betterment is concerned." [1]

The prevalent view of professional economists is that further encroachments upon the riches of the rich, by taxation or otherwise, will impair the incentive of the capitalists and entrepreneurs, so reducing the total product available for distribution, and that even were equalization of incomes possible, the quantity of surplus available (after adequate provision for savings) would not suffice to raise the mass of workers to an appreciably higher standard of living. Only by producing more and saving more can an aggregate income be got large enough to provide for a comfortable living with adequate leisure for a whole people. So far as the Christian Ethic is applicable, it tells the individual to work hard, produce more, and save more. This view differs not at all from the earlier Puritan teaching. Its address is directed to the individual. To industrial society, as a whole, it has little to say, for the conception of such a society lay outside the purview of Christ. Economic principles are only capable of modification to the extent that " the average standard of motive is changed "; and Christianity, in the West at any rate, has made no serious attempt to alter average standards of motive.

But while economists support the non-intervention of the Churches by saying there is very little they can do, and by suggesting that any sentimental interference with the working of economic laws would be either futile or disastrous, the churches on their part make no attempt to develop Gospel teaching into social-economic doctrines and policies that would be unpopular among their prominent supporters. The older standards of asceticism have disappeared from the Christian churches. The bicycle and the motor-car have almost destroyed sabbatarianism. Even in Scotland it becomes more difficult every year to maintain the dull austerity of the Calvinist sabbath. In England the ban upon Sunday games, secular music, reading, and other week-day occupations has in many places disappeared. Mammon is everywhere gaining ground, undermining not only the religious behaviour,

[1] *The Christian Ethic as an Economic Policy*, pp. **47–8**.

but also the beliefs of church members. Though the direct assaults of rationalism upon theology have doubtless played some part in this decay of theological beliefs, the indirect encroachments of " this world " have been of greater importance in promoting indifference to affairs of the next. It is not so much that positive disbelief in God and another world has displaced the old beliefs, but that the latter have been reduced to a tenuity which makes them no longer operative motives in conduct. This indifference is doubtless due in large measure to the utter failure of the Christian churches to cope with the great emergencies of life, to make a " gospel of peace " prevail when war is threatening, to curb the " will to power " in business or politics, and to protect the poor against their economic oppressors. In other words, the impotence of the Christian churches in handling issues of the gravest moral significance has brought them into something like contempt. There are large bodies of men and women both inside and outside the churches who realize this impotence. They do not become atheists, or necessarily abandon their formal church attachments. But church services, and the beliefs that are supposed to lie behind them, have become unreal, and for their canons of personal and social behaviour they look elsewhere. Not a few of the clergy recognize and deplore this situation. New grave issues regarding sex and population, art and literature, politics and industry, arise, and nobody expects the Christian churches to give out clear and useful utterances, or to influence public and private conduct.

Continental Socialism, as I have said, has definitely dissociated itself from Christianity, accepting Karl Marx's asseveration that " the idea of God must be destroyed : it is the keystone of a perverted civilization." Christianity belittles this world, preaches contentment, and serves as " the opium of the workers." Our own working-class and socialist movements have for the most part compromised here as on all critical issues. Just as the republicanism of Charles Bradlaugh died out of the radical secularism of the 'eighties with the revival of imperial sentimentalism, so his thoroughgoing atheism withered before the new wave of mysticism to which the most recent philosophy and science lend a helping hand. Partly, no doubt, it is a congenital distrust of reason as a sufficient guide to conduct, and a repudiation of " the falsehood of extremes." Englishmen are not prepared to hate or to destroy " the bourgeoisie." Their reason, their humour, and their humanity protect them against the violence of creed and behaviour to which Russian communism has succumbed.

To continental revolutionists this often appears as a " softness" of head and heart. And in a sense it is. But this " softness " has some place in the " common sense " which keeps us from extremes. " There was a time," writes Dr. Jacks, " when theology waxed eloquent over the total depravity of human nature. As much harm is done to-day by the doctrine of the total depravity of the social system." There can be no question that the full Socialist policy of the destruction of capitalism and the adoption of a complete state-Socialism has little purchase upon the minds of the masses of workers in this country, or of their leaders. There is no real belief in, or desire for, a "five-year plan " or any miraculous transformation of our economic system, though there is a keen, widespread desire for thoroughgoing changes in the control and working of industry, commerce, and finance, involving governmental or other representative control which shall secure regularity of employment and a reasonable progress in the standards of living, believed to be attainable by modern methods of production, with securities for a fair distribution of the product.

It is the almost complete failure of the churches to apply Christian ethics to the theory and practice of this reform policy that explains their loss of hold upon the people. For economic policy has assumed an intense consciousness in all classes within the last two generations. Its issues are grave both in themselves and in their hold upon the minds of the thinking section of every class. Now among leaders of the Christian churches, clergy or laymen, there are two widely divergent attitudes, though under pressure of controversy they may be taken by the same man in different circumstances.

The first and perhaps most widely held is that Christ's ethics do not contain principles for social conduct in business life. They are addressed to the individual soul. The purification of personal character expressed in conduct would doubtless evoke a social atmosphere of brotherly love that would express itself in friendly co-operation on the mundane plane. But the circumstances of Judaea in the time of Jesus were so remote from those which Mammon displays to-day as to make the simple general maxims of the Gospels inapplicable. " Love your neighbour as yourself " was a maxim feasible, though difficult of application, in a small local economic community where every buyer knew personally every seller, every lender every borrower, every worker every consumer. But in the intricacies of a highly organized national or world market, no man knows whom he serves or who consumes the goods to the making of which he contributes some fractional share. How, then, can the maxim of brotherly love be operative under such conditions? Co-operation has become an abstract term with hardly any personal content. This is perhaps what Dean Inge means when he says: "The standard in the Gospels is heroic and perfectionist; it is not, as we cannot remind ourselves too often, a code of permissible conduct for a large community."[1] It is apparently his disbelief in the willingness of people to accept from the Gospels their personal rules of conduct, including the disparagement of riches and of materialism in general, the neighbourly spirit, and all that goes with it, that makes him despondent of British Christianity. "The Christian Church suffers from what it is the fashion to call the inferiority complex. We are ashamed of being in a minority. We are distressed because our churches are half-empty. Many of them would be much emptier if the Gospel was preached in them."[2]

The deficient sociality of Christ's teaching and the emphasis upon purely personal conduct are reflected in the attitude adopted, not only by Dean Inge, but by most Christian Socialists, towards the economic problems of distribution. It would seem impossible for analysts of modern economic processes to deny that the moral gravamen of the charges against the inequity and human wastefulness of our economic system lies in the realm of distribution, the conditions and processes which determine how much of the " socially created product " shall go to the several owners of the instruments of production. Yet the avoidance of all close analytic scrutiny into distribution characterizes nearly all the economic pronouncements of theologians and church members. Here is a typical passage from a well-known American theologian, Professor Peabody:

" The fundamental evils of industrialism are not mechanical, but ethical; not primarily of the social order, but of the unsocialized soul. No rearrangement of production and distribution can of itself abolish the commercial instincts of ambition and competition, not even the baser desires of theft, covetousness, and deceit. A new order could not survive a year unless administered by unselfish minds and co-operative wills." So " the social order " is not conceived as " ethical," but as " mechanical " ! And mechanical changes of production and distribution cannot affect the soul or the ethics of the individual !

[1] *Christian Ethics and Modern Problems*, p. 67.
[2] *Op. cit.*, p. 392.

Hence it follows that the churches had best keep clear of proposed reforms of industry and the distribution of its product, and confine themselves to purifying the soul and will of man !

It does not seem to occur to such theologians that the economic environment may play an important part in moulding and stimulating the baser desires they deprecate, and in repressing the formation of " unselfish minds and co-operative wills." How can men love their neighbours, take no anxious thought for the morrow, co-operate with their fellows for the common good, within an economic system which operates, partly by competition, partly by private monopoly ? The " social order " is not mechanical, as Professor Peabody conceives it, but a bad moral order in which the thoughts and desires of men are directed to these selfish ends by the institutions that constitute that moral order. To tell men that the cultivation of personal virtues can release them from the injurious bondage of such an economic order is to talk sheer nonsense. So long as most men are kept struggling against one another for the bare materials of physical life, have no security for the continuous maintenance of themselves and their families, and little hope of improving their condition, they will remain selfish, greedy, covetous, deceitful.

It is doubtless true that " a new order "—a socialist or communist society—demands " unselfish minds and co-operative wills " for its successful working. But the formation of such a society would presuppose some measure of unselfishness and co-operative capacity, and its operation should confirm these qualities. Whatever may occur to the great experiment in Russia, it is unlikely that any Western people will evince so much unselfishness and co-operative will as to make a social reform on such a wholesale plan possible. But it might seem reasonable to expect that our clerical moralists, confronting the present instability of the social order in most countries of the world, would come to recognize that the political and economic institutions which largely constitute this order are proper material for their consideration. Instead, however, of realizing that these institutions are ethical in structure and in working, they still confine their attention to the purely personal factors in the social order.

This is why they have little concern for the productive processes in economic life, still less for distribution, and busy themselves almost entirely with consumption. For the consumer is the individualist in the economic system, and the persistent hankering after control of personal behaviour, which we have traced throughout the history of the Christian churches, survives to-day. If only people would not waste their money, their time, their health and energies, upon drink, gambling, and other light or baser amusements, they would have enough for all reasonable requirements and could save. They need not then entertain wicked notions of class war, strikes, or other disturbing enterprises !

This moral individualism of the churches is thus seen to ban enquiries into the equity and humanity of the distribution of income and property, by two methods of avoidance. The first is the treatment of wealth as a " trust " or " steward-ship," the origin of which is assumed to be the will of God, or the industry of the possessor. The second is the drawing away of thought from the producing processes into the con-suming. Not how wealth is got, but what is done with it when it is got, summarizes this convenient attitude.

Thus is brought about a new reconcilement between God and Mammon which is perhaps best expressed by an American millionaire in one of Joseph Hergesheimer's books : " Christian principles and American conceptions of business have put us where we are."

America, indeed, has developed the compromise into a positive co-partnership. Mammon is to have a free hand in the making, handing over to God (conceived as Church, University, Hospital, Library, or other instruments of the higher life) a quite considerable share of the spending. So if you are a church or a college, it is highly inconvenient that your clergy or your professors should poke their noses into the works, stores, banks, and markets from which emerge in some mysterious and intricate fashion the endowments and salaries which come to you from munificent donors. Therefore, you take care to discourage the nose-poking process. You also take care not to be conscious of these prohibitions, so that you may feel genuinely indignant when the charge is brought against you of discouraging freedom of economic thought and teaching. This is not hypocrisy, it is " rationalization " in the psychological sense of that word—i.e., finding a " good " reason for what you want to believe.

The dependence of the churches upon the superfluous incomes of the rich disables them from effective criticism of the sources of these incomes and from any serious attempt to probe into the causes of the poverty which they profess to deplore. Their general attitude towards unemployment is instructive. In a period of bad trade when many businesses

are dismissing employees, investigation of the character of
those who are " out " will indicate that they are usually less
efficient, less reliable, less sober, more feckless, than those who
have retained their jobs. Personal character is thus taken by
the church worker, or the C.O.S. investigator, to be the major
cause of unemployment. It is " the fault " of the unemployed
worker that he is unemployed. The assumption is that, if the
efficiency and moral character of these persons were raised to
the higher level of those who remain employed, they too would
have regular employment. Even those who are aware that
much unemployment is due to causes which lie outside the
responsibility of the worker or his employer, still entertain and
express the belief that a higher standard of industry, reliability,
thrift, and other personal factors would react upon the general
demand for labour so as to maintain it at a much higher level.
Now, though personal efficiency is a real factor in high produc-
tivity and low costs, there is no ground for holding that the
difference between the unemployed figures of 1920 and those
for 1930 is accounted for to any appreciable extent by these
personal factors.

Or take the more general attitude towards poverty. Because
the poor are upon an average less efficient workers and less
careful livers, poverty as such cannot be imputed to these
personal defects, though they determine to some extent who
shall be " the poor." Most of our city poor are born of poor
parents, bred in unhygienic surroundings, with poor food,
poor education, and poor training for the struggle of life.
These poor opportunities presuppose a poverty which is
attributable to prior inequality of economic opportunities—
i.e., the unjust distribution of property and of the advantages
it gives.

Now, if the churches really felt themselves the moral
guardians of the community, they would insist upon a full and
fearless exploration of the nature of the economic system in
its distributive capacity. They would then discover that the
conditions essential to " fair bargaining," just prices, equal
access to natural resources, to the use of capital, education,
and most opportunities of acquiring a comfortable and secure
living, were unattainable by the great majority of members of
the community. What the clerical moralist believes, in
common with most members of the well-to-do classes, is that
the economic system normally gives people " what they are
worth." It contains, indeed, some hardship and injustices,
and many mischances and breakdowns, that cause personal
distress. But the system of " capitalism " (competitive or

combinatory) is substantially sound; it delivers " the goods " better than any other system that can be devised. Some of its defects can be cured by better education, insurance, and other public services; others by the charity of those whose valuable services have brought them wealth !

A careful analysis of the arterial system of markets, the determination of the prices for the use of land, capital, ability, labour, the markets for food, raw materials, power, transport, finished goods, wholesale and retail, and last, but not least, the sale of credits and of stocks and shares—such analysis would disclose a moral obliquity in marketeering, a free play for selfish acquisitiveness, an habitual inequality in bargaining between buyer and seller, which would shock the conscience of the religious world. But motived by the considerations here indicated, the churches do not attempt this moral assay, they trust to the professors and the captains of industry, who assure them that this system works equitably " on the whole," and that no other system could succeed as well. To apply the maxims of Christ literally to modern business would be wholly impracticable, to attempt it would be to dry up the resources which are needed to maintain the churches and all other civilized institutions.

Now Western Christians are doubtless right in thinking that a strict application of the ethics of their religion, as expounded in the New Testament, would be incompatible with the acceptance of modern business methods. Nor, in fact, would it be compatible with the standards of values which regulate any other branch of our behaviour. The trouble lies deeper than any difficulty of squaring economic practices with Christian principles. Not merely the precepts but the ideals set out in the Gospels are repugnant to the Western mind. Meekness, love, or even forgiveness, of enemies, contempt for riches, disregard of the body, its food and raiment, have not been, and never will be, acceptable to any but tiny minorities in Western nations. Western ideals are more truthfully set forth in Malory's *Morte d'Arthur* than in the Gospels. It is true that chivalry was only the accepted ethic of a small master class, but it was the potential ethic of all the Western peoples, as the popular admiration for the sportsman, fighter, lover, adventurer, chieftain, testifies. It is this futile endeavour to fit an oriental, ascetic pacifism on to the Western temperament and valuations that baffles the comprehension of so many keen Eastern students of our civilization, often leading them to charge us with hypocrisy—a shallow rendering of the case.

Some years ago the Japanese Government sent to Europe a

commission to study religious institutions with a view to proposals for a religious reconstruction in Japan. The secretary, when asked by an Englishman whether the committee would advise the adoption of Christianity, replied : "That is impossible, for Christianity has been spoiled by occidentalism."

The Christian churches are, therefore, incapacitated from exercising moral influence over modern economic life, partly because their adherents do not seriously profess or apply the teaching of Christ, partly because they are aware that any attempt to apply it would fail and would quicken the process of dismemberment. A real Western religion, developed from pagan origins, and gradually spiritualized in accordance with the higher processes of civilization, in true organic relations with Western ideals and standards for intellectual and moral life, might have exercised a powerful " moulding " influence upon modern economic institutions, infusing into them the passion for fair play and equal opportunity, which is the essence of the " sportsman " spirit, together with the sense of comradeship capable of giving human significance to many of the otherwise mechanical processes of co-operation in economic life.

There is, however, a stronger case to be made for a religion, stripped of all theology and magic, that can supply this need, a definitely human religion which can apply to the support of our industrial and other institutions the principles and ideals of a rational ethic. There are moral individualists in the ranks of rationalism who shrink from all association with the name religion or the thing, who will make their own private settlement with ideals or standards of conduct. But there will be many others to whom this view is repugnant, especially in dealing with economic processes and activities that in their conduct and results are essentially corporate and co-operative. To an ever-increasing number of men and women of this temper and attitude the need for an organized ethical religion, based upon a rational interpretation of human progress in the arts of social life, will become the alternative to a selfish, mechanical determinism with no standard of values other than the urge of separate instincts and desires. The attainability of an effective religion of this order, holding together and inspiring by appeal to common needs and purposes the changeful wills of men, may remain a matter for legitimate doubt. But man is in many respects a more gregarious animal than ever, and in many ways of living is more and more assimilated to his fellows. In both his life and his work he can less than ever live unto himself alone. Although the value of his personality rests primarily in the ways in which he differs from his neighbours, the emergence and expression of that difference depend upon the strength and efficiency of the common human enterprise. And this common enterprise demands a willing co-operation of each man with the purposes and activities of his neighbours. Such social economics contains the essential character of a religion. For that character does not consist in a theology, but in the enthusiasm of humanity for a common and a worthy cause.

But though such co-operative zeal for human welfare is the kernel of a possible religion, it does not comprehend it. Hence ethics has not a monopoly of the religious sentiment. Science and philosophy set no such limit upon our interest. An attitude of curiosity and a feeling of community with nature in its widest sense are needed to complete the new structure of a rationalist religion. It was the failure of Positivism to include nature, save as a contribution towards the progress of humanity, that was responsible in part for the slight hold Comte and his disciples attained. But there was another reason for their failure, the parodying of Catholicism in its dogmatism and its ritual, with the creation of new saints and human demigods. Religion without theology, if it is to succeed, must take man's place in nature as its central theme. But it demands a recognition of nature as the larger and higher value. Nature does not exist to promote the ends of man alone, as the highest product. It is a great independent drama in which man plays a large, but not a separate and absorbing rôle.

A rationalist philosophy will not, therefore, I think, accept " Humanism " as an adequate religion. Still less will it accept the science and art of social economics as the chief goal of human striving. We have seen how throughout human history religions based upon spiritual or mystical pretensions have claimed to subdue Mammon, but Mammon has continually got the better in the conflict, inducing or compelling the organized churches to serve his economic ends. Now the world is offered in Bolshevism an inverted form of this experiment, where an economic Bible is substituted for the Christian book, and Marx and Lenin are objects of a genuine worship, the saints of a new social order, which utilizes all the devices of the old religions, including the apocalyptic vision of a millennium of prosperity following a few years of trial and fasting. A distinctively religious attitude of adoration of the State, its will and its perfectibility, is promoted by a propaganda presenting all the features of a religious revivalism. This God-State is as arbitrary in its will, as repressive of private liberty of thought and action, as cruel in its persecuting zeal, as any of the spiritual deities that have preceded it. Whether regarded as a political or an economic religion, it is as abhorrent to Rationalism as any of the preposterous theologies it seeks to displace.

A rationalist religion would not commit the fatal error of conceiving body and spirit as ultimately separate and opposed in character and aims. Nor would it achieve a unity by allowing the one to deny the reasonable claims, or even the real existence, of the other, under such alternatives as Idealism and Materialism. It would conceive man, individual and collective, as the most finely composed part of nature, directed in his behaviour by a more definitely conscious urge than is discernible in the rest of the animate world. That urge in man such a religion would claim to be rational, in that its function is, first, to establish, not for all time but for humanity in its present situation, some standard of values, some ideal of a good life, then to direct the otherwise unrelated or conflicting instincts and desires towards the achievement of this ideal. This process would be in substance an enlightened utilitarianism, in which bodily satisfactions would have their proper place along with spiritual, under a system of thought in which the division of body and spirit is not regarded as an ultimate division of nature. Thus the bickering of God and Mammon would cease, and religion and economics would achieve a serviceable co-operation, in a world where it was made possible for everyone to " keep body and soul together."

For Product Safety Concerns and Information please contact our EU
representative GPSR@taylorandfrancis.com Taylor & Francis Verlag GmbH,
Kaufingerstraße 24, 80331 München, Germany

Printed and bound by CPI Group (UK) Ltd, Croydon, CR0 4YY
02/05/2025
01859316-0001